English for Business Communication

Second Edition

A short course consisting of five modules:
Cultural diversity and socialising, Telephoning,
Presentations, Meetings and Negotiations

Student's Book

Simon Sweeney

CAMBRIDGE
UNIVERSITY PRESS

CAMBRIDGE UNIVERSITY PRESS
Cambridge, New York, Melbourne, Madrid, Cape Town, Singapore, São Paulo, Delhi

Cambridge University Press
The Edinburgh Building, Cambridge CB2 8RU, UK

www.cambridge.org
Information on this title: www.cambridge.org/9780521754491

First published 1997
Second Edition 2003
8th printing 2009

Printed in Dubai by Oriental Press

A catalogue record for this publication is available from the British Library

ISBN 978-0-521-75449-1 Student's Book
ISBN 978-0-521-75450-7 Teacher's Book
ISBN 978-0-521-75451-4 Audio Cassette Set
ISBN 978-0-521-75452-1 Audio CD

Contents

Introduction to the second edition

English for Business Communication is a short course with two key objectives:

- to develop your technique in five key areas of communication: socialising, telephoning, presenting information, participating in meetings and negotiations
- to develop your knowledge of the language used in these key areas.

The course is concerned with improving your listening and speaking skills. There is a lot of opportunity to practise understanding from the recorded material. It is important that you try to understand the key message of the extracts, not every word you hear. Similarly, there are several reading texts where again you should try to understand the key messages, not necessarily every word on the page.

There are very many opportunities for discussion and plenty of role plays. The discussion is partly designed to get you to think about what makes communication effective. The practice material and the role plays lead to a Transfer exercise. This is a chance to connect what you have studied with your own daily experience, either as a student or as a professional working in business. The skills learned from this course are useful for those preparing to start work and for those already in work.

As you use the course, practise as much as you can and prepare for meetings, presentations or telephone calls by using the Checklists at the end of each unit. Always refer to these when preparing a communication task. Try to develop the habit of good preparation. Try also to develop the habit of self-assessment to help you to see where improvements can be made. Your teacher will help you with this.

Enjoy the course!

This second edition not only provides improvements to the overall appearance and design of the book, but also responds to users' requests for more practice material. There is now an additional page of exercises summarising key language from each unit (Quick Communication Check), designed for self-study use. The listening material has been extensively re-recorded with improvements throughout. Together with various small changes, much of the practice material has also been updated.

Simon Sweeney

MODULE 1

CULTURAL DIVERSITY AND SOCIALISING

1 Building a relationship

AIMS

- Cross-cultural understanding (1)
- Welcoming visitors
- Small talk: keeping the conversation going

1 Cross-cultural understanding (1)

1 **Look at the picture. In groups, discuss the situation. Decide what you think the people are talking about. Suggest various topics. Say what you think they are definitely *not* talking about. Then spend a few minutes acting out the conversation.**

2 **Read the text below. Identify the basic message implied by the text.**

Eye contact

In many Western societies, including the United States, a person who does not maintain 'good eye contact' is regarded as being slightly suspicious, or a 'shifty' character. Americans unconsciously associate people who avoid eye contact as unfriendly, insecure, untrustworthy, inattentive and impersonal. However, in contrast, Japanese children are taught in school to direct their gaze at the region of their teacher's Adam's apple or tie knot, and, as adults, Japanese lower their eyes when speaking to a superior, a gesture of respect.

Latin American cultures, as well as some African cultures, such as Nigeria, have longer looking time, but prolonged eye contact from an individual of lower status is considered disrespectful. In the US, it is considered rude to stare – regardless of who is looking at whom. In contrast, the polite Englishman is taught to pay strict attention to a speaker, to listen carefully, and to blink his eyes to let the speaker know he or she has been understood as well as heard. Americans signal interest and comprehension by bobbing their heads or grunting.

A widening of the eyes can also be interpreted differently, depending on circumstances and culture. Take, for instance, the case of an American and a Chinese discussing the terms of a proposed contract. Regardless of the language in which the proposed contract is carried out, the US negotiator may interpret a Chinese person's widened eyes as an expression of astonishment instead of as a danger signal (its true meaning) of politely expressed anger.

Adapted from *Managing Cultural Differences, Fourth Edition,* by Phillip R. Harris and Robert T. Moran.

3 If necessary, read the text again. Then comment on the following:

a) observations about many people from the United States
b) observations about the English
c) an observation about Japanese children
d) the meaning of lowering one's eyes in Japan
e) why looking at someone for a long time may be considered disrespectful
f) the meaning of widened eyes in Chinese culture.

4 Before receiving a visitor from a foreign country – or before travelling abroad – you need to think about the cultural issues that may affect the relationship.

a) Suggest some basic research that you should do before receiving your visitor, or before travelling. What issues should you think about?

Note: After suggesting your own ideas, compare your list with the Skills Checklist at the end of this unit.

b) Listen to the recording. An American, Peter Wasserman, who is the CEO of an international company, talks about what he thinks is important in preparing for business contacts with people from other cultures. He mentions several key areas to find out about. Identify six of them. Did you think of any of the same issues?

Discussion

In what way is the advice in this section useful when doing business? Look again at the Skills Checklist on page 12.

2 Welcoming visitors

What happens when a visitor arrives with an appointment to visit a company? What are the typical stages of the first meeting? What conversations take place?

1 **Listen to the recording in which Klaus Ervald arrives for a meeting with Lars Elstroem and Louise Scott of Evco S.A., a Swedish advertising agency.**

a) Is the meeting between Klaus Ervald and Evco formal or informal? Give reasons for your answer.
b) Do they know each other quite well?
c) Klaus has a problem. What is it?

2 **Listen again. Think again about how Louise and Lars talk to Klaus.**
She interrupts him at the start. Is this acceptable?
They use first names. Is this right, given the situation?
Lars begins to talk about the programme for the day. Is this appropriate at this stage?

3 **Listen to the recording of Peter Marwood's arrival at SDA Ltd., in Sydney, Australia. He has to wait a few minutes and asks Stephanie Field for some assistance. Identify two things he needs and three things he does not need.**

Needs

a) send email
b) send some flowers to ex-wife

Does not need

c) coffee
d) read - economist
e) cap

I need to send ...

Practice 1

Make a dialogue based on the following flow chart. If you need help, look at the Language Checklist on page 12.

Visitor	Receptionist
Introduce yourself.	
Say you have an appointment with Sandra Bates.	
	Welcome visitor.
	Explain that SB will be along shortly.
	Offer a drink / refreshments.
Decline – ask if you can use a phone.	
	Say yes. / Offer email as well.
Decline – you only need the phone.	
	Show visitor to the phone.
Thank him / her.	
(*a few minutes later*)	
Thank assistant.	
	Reply – offer any other help.
Ask how far it is to station.	
	Two miles – ten minutes by taxi.
	Offer to book one.
Accept offer – suggest a time.	
	Promise to do that – say that SB is free now.
	Offer to take him / her to SB's office.

Now listen to the recording of a model answer.

3 Small talk: keeping the conversation going

1 Ruud Hemper from the Netherlands is visiting a customer in India. He is talking to the Production Manager of a manufacturing plant in Delhi. Listen to the recording of an extract of their conversation.

MANAGER: Is this your first visit here?

HEMPER: No, in fact the first time I came was for a trade fair. We began our Southeast Asian operations here at the 2003 Exhibition.

MANAGER: Shall we have a look round the plant before lunch?

a) What is wrong with what the Production Manager says?
The answer is, of course, that it breaks a 'rule' of conversation. Generally, if you ask a question you should comment on the answer or ask a supplementary question.

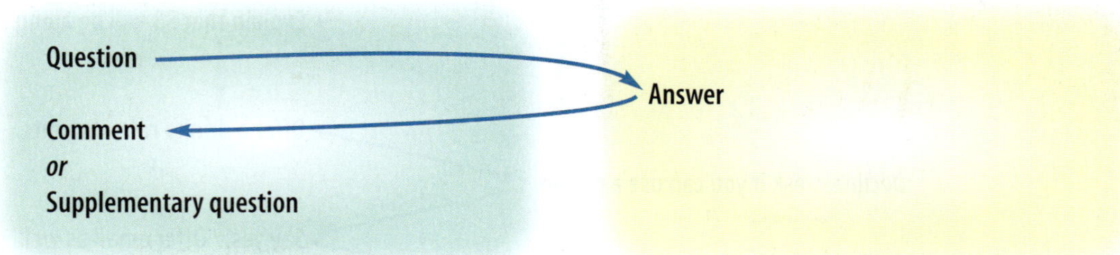

b) Now suggest a better version of the same conversation. There is a recording of a model version.

2 Provide a suitable sentence in the spaces in the following dialogue.

PETER: Have you been to Edinburgh before?

JANIS: No, it's my first visit.

PETER: (a) ....

JANIS: I'm sure I will.

PETER: And … er, is the hotel all right?

JANIS: Yes, it's very comfortable.

PETER: (b) .... So, do you have much time here in Scotland? Are you staying long?

JANIS: No, I have to go back tomorrow afternoon.

PETER: (c) .... You'll have to come back again!

JANIS: (d) ....

PETER: So what time's your flight tomorrow?

JANIS: Early evening, 18.35.

PETER: Well, I can book you a taxi if you like, to get you there in good time.

JANIS: (e) ....

PETER: No problem at all. Was it a good flight today?

JANIS: No, it wasn't actually.

PETER: (f) .... (g) .... ?

JANIS: It was raining – quite hard. There was a lot of turbulence.

PETER: (h) ....

3 **Listen to the recording of four conversation extracts.**

a) Match each of them to one of the four pictures below.

b) Listen to each one again. In each case, suggest how you think the conversation might develop.

c) Do you think any of the topics included would be unacceptable in a particular culture that you know about?

Practice 2

Look at the four pictures above and use each of them for two or three minutes of continual conversation with a partner.

Note:

- there should be no breaks of more than three seconds in your conversation
- listen carefully to what your partner says and pick up on specific points
- keep the conversation flowing.

Role play 1

Working in pairs. Student A should look at File card 1A and Student B should look at File card 1B.

Role play 2

Keep the same A and B. Student A should look at File card 2A. Student B should look at File card 2B.

TRANSFER

Look at the Skills Checklist and prepare ideas on these topics in relation to a country you know well either through work or pleasure.
Discuss the country you choose with a colleague.

Language Checklist

Cultural diversity and socialising (1)

Welcoming visitors
Welcome to …
My name's …

Arriving
Hello. My name's … from …
I've an appointment to see …
Sorry – I'm a little late / early.
My plane was delayed …

Introducing someone
This is … He / She's my Personal Assistant.
Can I introduce you to … He / She's our (Project Manager).
I'd like to introduce you to …

Meeting someone and small talk
Pleased to meet you.
It's a pleasure.
How was your trip? Did you have a good flight / trip / journey?
How are things in (London)?
How long are you staying in (New York)?
I hope you like it.
Is your hotel comfortable?
Is this your first visit to (Berlin)?

Offering assistance
Can I get you anything?
Do you need anything?
Would you like a drink?
If you need to use a phone or fax, please say.
Can we do anything for you?
Do you need a hotel / a taxi / any travel information / etc.?

Asking for assistance
There is one thing I need …
Could you get me …
Could you book me a car / taxi / hotel / … ?
Could you help me arrange a flight to … ?
Can you recommend a good restaurant?
I'd like to book a room for tomorrow night. Can you recommend a hotel?

Skills Checklist

Socialising (1)

Before meeting business partners and fellow professionals from other countries, you could find out about their country:

- the actual political situation
- cultural and regional differences
- religion(s)
- the role of women in business and in society as a whole
- transport and telecommunications systems
- the economy
- the main companies
- the main exports and imports
- the market for the industrial sector which interests you
- competitors.

You might also want to find out:

- which topics are safe for small talk
- which topics are best avoided.

If you are going to visit another country, find out about:

- the conventions regarding socialising
- attitudes towards foreigners
- attitudes towards gifts
- the extent to which public, business and private lives are mixed or are kept separate
- conventions regarding food and drink.

You might also like to find out about:

- the weather at the relevant time of the year
- public holidays
- the conventions regarding working hours
- leisure interests
- tourism
- dress
- body language
- language.

Quick Communication Check

1 Welcoming visitors

Complete the dialogue with words from the box.

A: Hello, (a) .... to meet you.
B: Thank you for (b) .... me.
A: How long are you (c) .... here?
B: Just two days.
A: Oh, not long, then. Let me (d) .... you to my colleague Paul.
B: Paul, (e) .... is Angela Fox.

this	staying	nice	introduce	inviting

2 Making small talk

Match the phrases 1–5 to the correct responses a–e to make a conversation.

1 Did you have a good trip?
2 Was the flight on time?
3 That's good. And how was the weather in London?
4 Really? Well it's much better here.
5 Can I get you a drink or something?

a) Very wet and cold, I'm afraid.
b) Yes, it was.
c) Thank you. A coffee would be great.
d) Very good, thank you.
e) Yes, it's very warm.

3 Asking for and giving help

Classify the sentences below into offering something (O), declining an offer (D), asking for help (H), accepting an offer (A).

a) Can I get you anything?
b) No, I'm fine thanks.
c) Just a question, is there a chemist's near here?
d) Would you like a drink, tea or coffee?
e) Yes, maybe … a cold drink, if I may.
f) Can I use your phone?
g) I'd like to print something from this disk, if possible.
h) Would you like a lift to your hotel?

Key
1 (a) nice, (b) inviting, (c) staying, (d) introduce, (e) this
2 1 d), 2 b), 3 a), 4 e), 5 c)
3 a) (O), b) (D), c) (H), d) (O), e) (A), f) (H), g) (H), h) (O)

2 Culture and entertainment

AIMS

- Cross-cultural understanding (2)
- Inviting, and accepting or declining
- Eating out

1 Cross-cultural understanding (2)

1 **The following text is about cultural diversity. Read it through once and decide which of the three statements (A, B or C) given below the extract offers the most accurate summary.**

The impact of culture on business

Take a look at the new breed of international managers, educated according to the most modern management philosophies. They all know that in the SBU, TQM should reign, with products delivered JIT, where CFTs distribute products while subject to MBO. (SBU = strategic business unit, TQM = total quality management, JIT = just-in-time, CFT = customer first team, MBO = management by objectives.)

But just how universal are these management solutions? Are these 'truths' about what effective management really is: truths that can be applied anywhere, under any circumstances?

Even with experienced international companies, many well-intended 'universal' applications of management theory have turned out badly. For example, pay-for-performance has in many instances been a failure on the African continent because there are particular, though unspoken, rules about the sequence and timing of reward and promotions. Similarly, management by objectives schemes have generally failed within subsidiaries of multinationals in southern Europe, because managers have not wanted to conform to the abstract nature of preconceived policy guidelines.

Even the notion of human-resource management is difficult to translate to other cultures, coming as it does from a typically Anglo-Saxon doctrine. It borrows from economics the idea that human beings are 'resources' like physical and monetary resources. It tends to assume almost unlimited capacities for individual development. In countries without these beliefs, this concept is hard to grasp and unpopular once it is understood. International managers have it tough. They must operate on a number of different premises at any one time. These premises arise from their culture of origin, the culture in which they are working, and the culture of the organisation which employs them.

In every culture in the world such phenomena as authority, bureaucracy, creativity, good fellowship, verification and accountability are experienced in different ways. That we use the same words to describe them tends to make us unaware that our cultural biases and our accustomed conduct may not be appropriate, or shared.

From *Riding the Waves of Culture: Understanding Cultural Diversity in Business* by Fons Trompenaars, Irwin Professional Publishing, Burr Ridge, Illinois 1994.

A There are certain popular universal truths about management which can successfully be applied in various cultural contexts.

B Cultures are so varied and so different throughout the world that management has to take account of differences rather than simply assume similarities.

C Effective management of human resources is the key to everyone achieving their full potential.

2 **Read the text again. Identify the following:**

a) the problem with 'universal' management solutions
b) an example of the failure of pay-for-performance
c) an example of the failure of management by objectives schemes
d) the problem with human-resource management
e) three cultures affecting international managers
f) six areas in which different cultural interpretations apply.

2 Inviting, and accepting or declining

What kinds of social activities in your town could be appropriate ways of entertaining visitors from other countries?

1 **Listen to the first example on the recording. You will hear a conversation in which someone invites a business associate to a social event. Identify:**

a) what is being suggested
b) the response
c) what will happen next.

2 **Listen to the second example, where someone else invites a different business associate to a social event. Identify:**

a) what is being suggested
b) the response
c) what will happen next.

3 Listen to the recording of three short extracts, where hosts invite their visitors to take part in a social activity. The invitations are rejected.

a) Identify each suggested activity.
b) Give the reasons for each rejection.
c) Do you think each rejection is appropriate? Explain your answer.

Activity	Reason for rejection	Comments
1		
2		
3		

4 Work in pairs. Use the advertisements below to invite your partner to something. He/she should respond. Then change roles so you both get to invite and accept or reject in each situation.

a) tomorrow night / a show or visit the town / or have a meal.
b) this evening / a meal in a restaurant / different colleagues.
c) when you come / what would you like to do?

City Museum & Art Gallery
Drawings from the Italian Renaissance
The Stenwald Collection of drawings by masters of the Renaissance including Bernini, Leonardo da Vinci, Michelangelo, Tiepolo, Titian, Vasari.
April 3rd – July 24th
Admission 10 a.m. – 9 p.m.
Museum Square Tel 0467 987 785

Art House Cinema
20–24 Copper Street
Screen One: The Enigma of Kaspar Hauser
Director Werner Herzog starring Bruno S., Eva Mattes, Clemens Scheitz.
Screen Two: Once Upon a Time in the West
Director Sergio Leone starring Henry Fonda, Charles Bronson, Claudia Cardinale.
All this week: 9.00.
Booking 020 7857 8211

Guido Fornaro Concert Hall
City University Orchestra
Kohei Yamamoto (Conductor)
Franz Stefenberg (Piano)
Stravinsky *Firebird Suite (1945)*
Bartók *Piano Concerto No 3*
Kurtág *Stele, Op.33 Four Capriccios Op.9*
Wednesday and Thursday 7.30 p.m.
Box Office 020 7834 2288
www.cc.ac.org/univ/concert/ (no booking fee)

Studio Theatre, Sheep Street
The Cherry Orchard
Anton Chekov
Directed by Anatole Pier Martinov
Every night at 8.30 p.m.
All prices available.
Student nights Mondays and Tuesdays.
'Marvellous, timeless theatre' City Gazette
'Russian drama at its best' Time In Reviews
'Brilliant' The Stage

PAVILION MUSIC HOUSE
88 Lime St
Night Music & Lights
The best in contemporary dance music
plus top local live bands
House DJ Mixer Mo
Admission includes two drinks
(see website for details)
www.pavilion.com

City Opera House
SOUTH PARADE
NORTHERN TOURING OPERA
Bizet's Carmen
New production directed by Colin Makepiece
'A new force in opera' Classical Review
'Superb design and passionate performances' The Guide

Finally, listen to the recording of model versions.

Practice

1 Use the following flow chart to construct a dialogue. The situation is a semi-formal business meeting in your country.

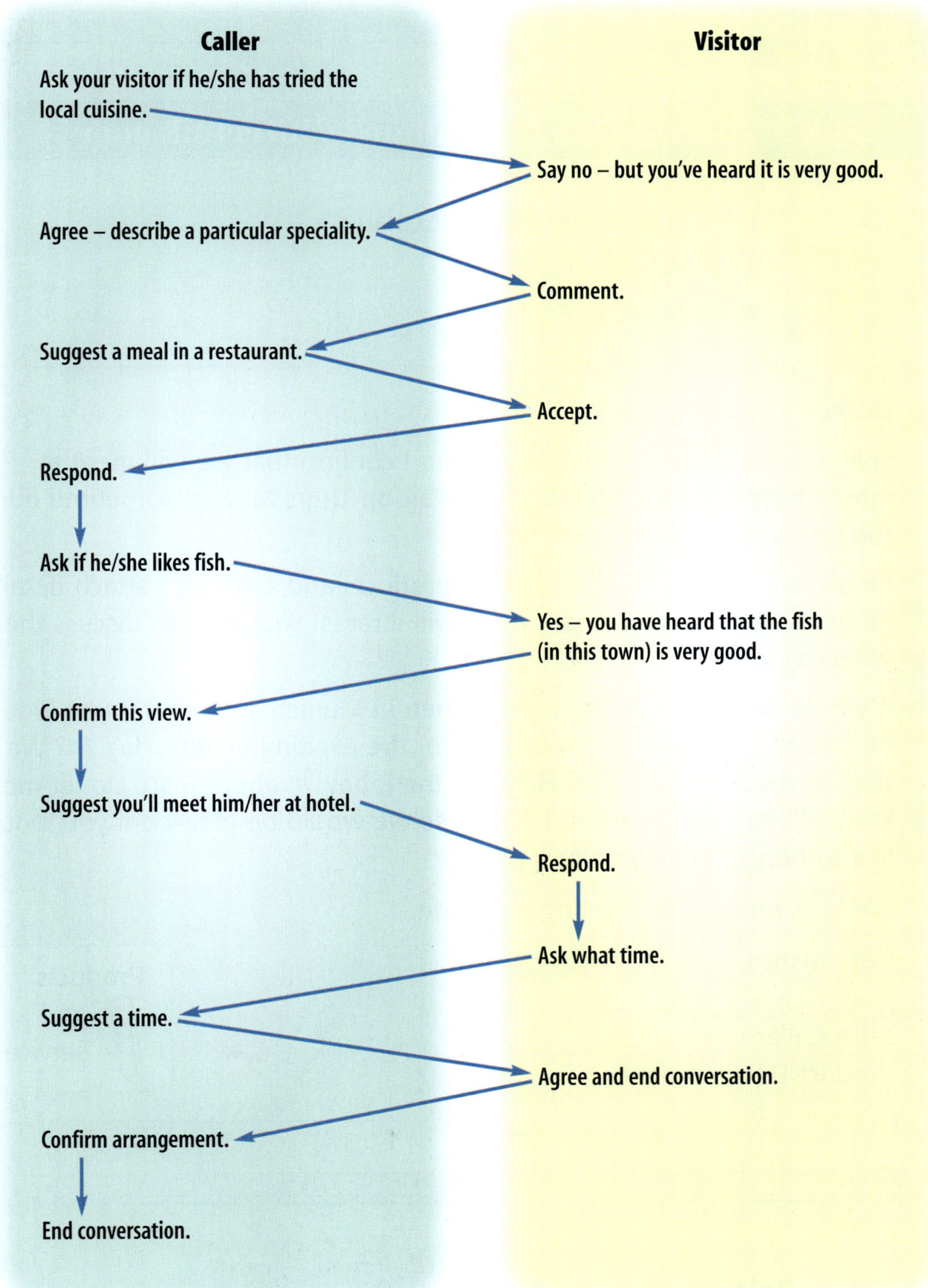

Now listen to the recording of a model answer.

2 You receive the email below from a business partner confirming a meeting with you at a trade fair in Munich. Unfortunately you have to leave Munich after your meeting, but you expect to be in London a week later. Write a reply suggesting a different arrangement which you can confirm nearer the time.

Main identity

FROM "John Callam" <jcallam2@interlink.com

TO m.j.saans.accounts@saboc.co.au

SENT 15 March 20–10.38

Subject **Munich Trade Fair**

Maria,

Following our telephone conversation I confirm that we will meet at Interlink stand at the Munich Trade Fair on Thurs May 24 sometime during the morning.

I look forward to talking about our products and services. I attach details of some new products that I think will interest you. We can discuss these when we meet.

It would be nice to meet socially when in Munich. I wonder if you would be free to join me and a colleague for the evening of Thursday 24? We plan to meet at the Hilton Hotel, in the lobby, at about 8.30. Do let me know if you can join us and of course we would be pleased if you would like to bring a colleague or a partner.

We look forward to meeting you soon.

Best wishes,

John Callam
Product Development

Products and services

100% Page: 1

Role play 1

Work in pairs. Student A should look at File card 3A. Student B should look at File card 3B.

3 Eating out

1 **Imagine you are in a restaurant with a business colleague. Work in groups of three. Brainstorm as many examples as you can of the language indicated below.**

Group one
recommending what to eat   expressing preference   ordering

Group two
commenting on the food   asking for the bill   offering to pay

Group three
insisting on paying   inviting   thanking

2 **Divide into fresh groups of three and together in your new groups share all the examples you have of different ways of saying the nine functions above.**

Complete the grid below with possible phrases:

Recommending what to eat	**Expressing preference**	**Ordering**
Commenting on the food	**Asking for the bill**	**Offering to pay**
Insisting on paying	**Inviting**	**Thanking**

3 Now listen to a conversation recorded in a restaurant. The recording contains parts of a conversation between Patricia Cork and Sandra Martinez. They are colleagues in a joint venture between two American companies.

Note any similarities between your suggestions and the language in the recording. Note also any phrases used on the tape that you did not suggest.

Role play 2

Student A should turn to File card 4A and Student B should turn to File card 4B.

TRANSFER

Think of any professional or business contact you have with other countries. Think about any conventions that are different from those in your country and may affect your dealings with people from these countries. Consider for example:

- conventions of dress
- conventions regarding alcohol and food
- socialising
- shaking hands
- physical contact
- gestures
- eye contact
- humour
- the relationship between work and pleasure
- the relationship between family and work
- family matters.

Language Checklist

Socialising (2)

Saying what's on and what's available
There's a (good) film / play / concert / on at …
We have a good theatre in the city …
There are some …
– interesting museums / public buildings …
– good restaurants
Are you interested in …
– eating out?
– visiting / seeing … ?

Inviting
Would you be interested in going to see … ?
I'd like to invite you to have dinner this evening. Is that a good idea?

Responding to an invitation
That would be very nice.
I'd like that.
Thank you. That would be a pleasure.

Declining an invitation
I'd like to, but I'm afraid …
That would be nice, but unfortunately …
– I'm rather tired …
– I have an appointment this evening …
– I'm rather busy …
– I have some work to do …

Stating preference
I like (Japanese) cuisine very much …
I think I'd like to …
I think I'd prefer …
I particularly like (classical) music …

Looking at a menu
The (fish) sounds nice …
I think I'd like to try …
I think I'll have …
Shall we have a bottle of … ?

Commenting on an evening out
It's been a lovely evening.
It's been very nice.
Thank you very much for your hospitality.
I enjoyed it very much.

Skills Checklist

Socialising (2)

Before receiving visitors to your company, be prepared to talk in English about your professional field and / or your company and business:

- the professional field you are involved in
- your professional activities
- current research and other projects
- future plans
- the history of your company
- company organisation
- who owns the company
- the number of employees
- the international involvement of your company
- products and services
- the market
- competition.

Be able to talk about:

- your country and your town
- history
- tourism
- museums and public buildings
- entertainment
- cultural and religious centres of interest.

You may wish to talk about:

- education
- transport systems
- the economy
- companies
- exports and imports.

Quick Communication Check

1 Inviting

Choose the correct ending to make the invitations below.

1 Do you have any	a) to meet this evening?
2 There's a good	b) free time this week?
3 We could go for	c) you some interesting places.
4 Would you like	d) museum near here.
5 I'd like to show	e) a meal in a restaurant.

2 Accepting or declining

A Which of these words indicate an acceptance (A) of an invitation? Which words indicate a rejection (R) of an invitation?

nice idea | very kind | unfortunately | rather busy | have to
thank you, but | I'm sorry | excellent | very kind

B Complete the sentences below with words from the box.

a) I'd like that .... unfortunately I .... leave very early in the morning.
b) That's very .... of you, I'd .... that very much.
c) Thank you, that .... be very interesting.
d) It is nice of you to .... me, but I already have an .... tonight. I'm sorry about that.
e) Another .... perhaps?
f) I'd like ...., thank you very much.

time
kind
but
have to
would
invite
appointment
that
like

3 Eating out

Make correct sentences from the jumbled words below.

a) the can menu have I please
b) I'd start like soup please vegetable to with
c) casserole have I'll chicken then
d) a the water and of please côtes-du-rhône mineral bottle
e) a may bill I have the coffee and please

Key

1 1b), 2d), 3e), 4a) 5c)

2
A
nice idea (A), very kind (A), unfortunately (R), rather busy (R), have to (R), thank you, but (R), I'm sorry (R), excellent (A), very kind (A)

B
a) but, have to, b) kind, like, c) would, d) invite, appointment, e) time, f) that

3 a) Can I have the menu, please?
b) I'd like to start with vegetable soup, please.
c) Then I'll have chicken casserole
d) The côtes-du-rhône and a bottle of mineral water, please.
e) May I have a coffee and the bill, please.

MODULE 2

TELEPHONING

3 Could I leave a message?

AIMS

- Preparing to make a telephone call
- Receiving calls
- Taking and leaving messages
- Asking for and giving repetition
- The secretarial barrier

1 Preparing to make a telephone call

1 Look at the cartoon. What do you imagine they are saying? Say what the problems are and how problems like this can be avoided.

2 Listen to the recording of Clare Macey, a director of Inter Marketing, suggesting ways to prepare for telephone calls. Then tick the suggestions that she makes that are included in the list below.

Do *not* try to guess what the other person will say. ☐

Think about your objectives from the call – any questions you need to ask or things you need to say. ☐

If someone calls and you are not ready for them, ask them to call back later. ☐

Desk preparation: prepare the desk – paper, pen, any relevant documentation, computer files. ☐

Check recent correspondence, know the situation. ☐

Have your diary on hand, so you can fix appointments. ☐

3 **Different people have different objectives in a telephone call. What do you think are the objectives of the people in the situations below? The first is done for you as an example.**

a) A purchasing manager who has received an incomplete delivery.

- *To tell the supplier that the delivery is incomplete.*
- *To arrange to get the rest of the delivery sent as soon as possible.*
- *(Possibly) to complain about the poor service.*

b) A computer operator with a software problem calling a software helpline.

c) A sales representative for a furniture manufacturer making a first call to Moda Design, a company which sells office furniture.

d) A purchaser at Moda Design who takes the call in situation c.

2 Receiving calls

1 **Look at the picture as you listen to the recording. Say what the problem is and how problems like this can be avoided.**

2 Listen to another short extract from the recording of Clare Macey. Here she is talking about being prepared for incoming calls. Tick what she recommends.

Send an email suggesting someone calls you – then be prepared for their call.	☐
If you expect a call, think about what the other person will say or what they will ask.	☐
Check any relevant documentation or correspondence.	☐
If you are busy or not ready when they call, ask them to call back later.	☐

3 Taking and leaving messages

1 Listen to the recording and write key information on the message pads below.

a)

PHONE MEMO

TO	DATE	TIME AM PM
FROM	AREA CODE NO.	
OF	EXT.	

MESSAGE

SIGNED

PHONED ☐ CALL BACK ☐ RETURNED CALL ☐ WANTS TO SEE YOU ☐ WILL CALL AGAIN ☐ WAS IN ☐ **URGENT** ☐

b)

Telephone Messages

To ______ Date ______

From ______ Time ______

Of ______ Phone ______ / ______
AREA CODE/NUMBER

Message

______

Signed ______

Discussion

Compare the styles of the callers in the two conversations you have heard. How are they different? Comment on how the people answering the calls handle each caller.

Now listen to two more examples and complete the message pads below.

c)

TO: ______________________ ❑ URGENT
DATE ______________________ TIME ________

WHILE YOU WERE OUT

M ______________________
OF ______________________
PHONE ______________________
AREA NUMBER EXTENSION

❑ TELEPHONED ❑ PLEASE CALL
❑ CAME TO SEE YOU ❑ WILL CALL AGAIN
❑ WANTS TO SEE YOU ❑ RETURNED YOUR CALL

MESSAGE ______________________

SIGNED ______________________

d)

Computer Services User Support

TO ______________________
FROM ______________________
TIME ______________________
EXTENSION ______________________
DEPARTMENT ______________________
WORKSTATION ______________________
NOTES

Problem/enquiry:

Discussion

Discuss the style of the various speakers in the last two conversations. How does the style change according to the speaker and the situation? Is the style used always the right one?

Practice

Use the following flow chart to make a complete telephone conversation. If you need to, listen again to the recordings you have heard and refer to the Language Checklist on page 32.

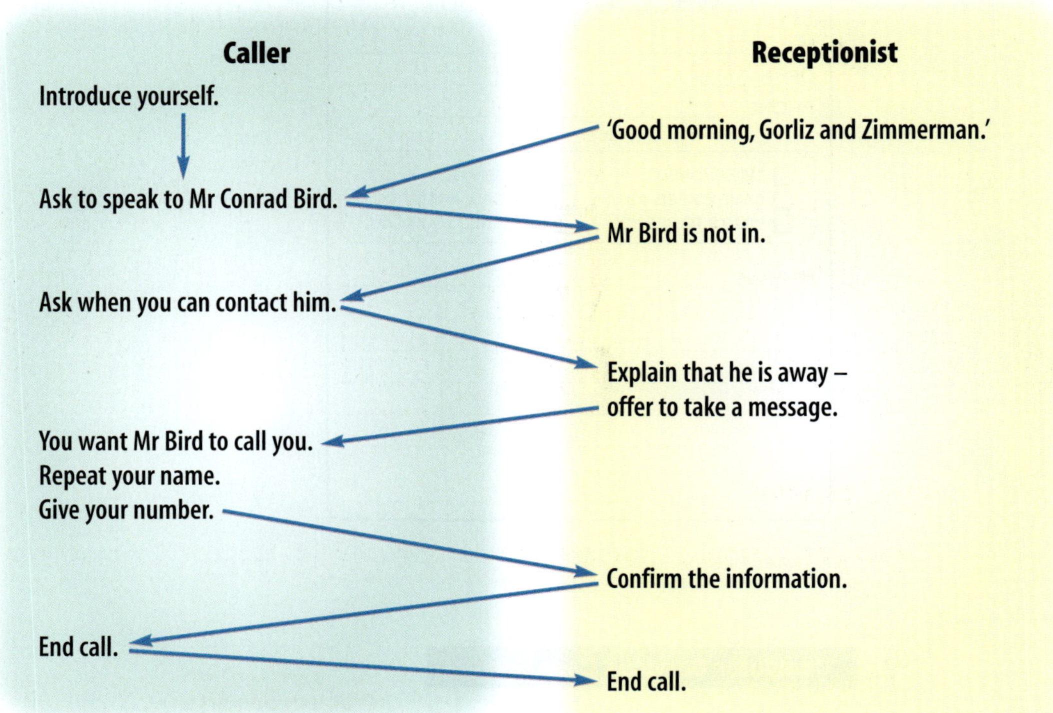

Now listen to the recording of a model answer.

4 Asking for and giving repetition

1 **Listen to the recording of a conversation between a woman who calls the Human Resources Office in the Singapore branch of Michigan Insurance Inc. She has to attend for a job interview.**
   a) The first time you listen, say why she calls.
   b) Listen again. Notice that there are four requests for repetition. Why?

2 **In each request for repetition, the person asking for the repetition also acknowledges it. It is important that any repetition is followed by an acknowledgement. Look at the following example that you have heard:**

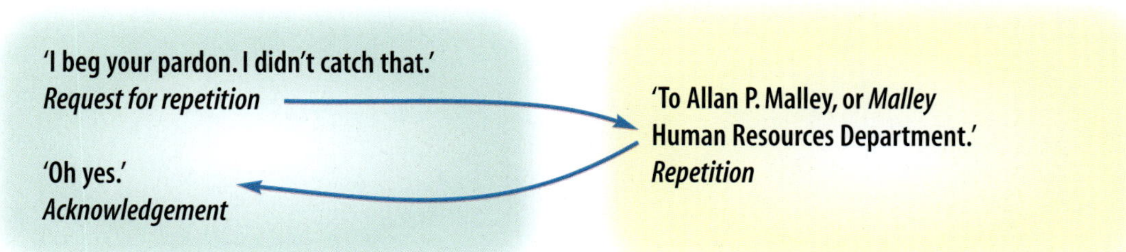

Listen again. Identify two other ways to acknowledge repetition.

3 Look at the following situations and listen to the recording for each one. In each case, suggest why someone might ask for repetition and suggest a suitable phrase.

1

2

3

Role play 1

Work in pairs. Student A should turn to File card 5A. Student B should turn to File card 5B.

Role play 2

Keep to the same A or B. Student A should turn to File card 6A and Student B should turn to File card 6B.

5 The secretarial barrier

1 Frequently a sales representative may make a 'cold call' to a purchasing manager or some other influential person in a company. Imagine the following situation:

Dominique Peron is Personal Assistant to Jacques Le Grand, Production Controller in Compagnie Tarbet Garonne (CTG), a French manufacturer of paints and varnishes. M. Le Grand has asked not to be disturbed by uninvited sales calls. Walter Barry from London would like to speak to M. Le Grand.

a) Listen to the tape and say what Dominique is trying to do. What is her objective?
b) Dominique Peron finally makes a suggestion to the caller. What does she say?

2 Listen again. Complete the script below by writing down all the phrases used by Dominique Peron to block the caller.

CTG: Bonjour, ici la CTG.

WALTER BARRY: Good morning, Walter Barry, here, calling from London. Could I speak to M. Le Grand, please?

CTG: Who's calling, please?

WALTER BARRY: I'm sorry – Walter Barry, from London.

CTG: Er, ..., please?

WALTER BARRY: Well, I understand that your company has a chemical processing plant. My own company, LCP, Liquid Control Products, is a leader in safety in the field of chemical processing. I would like to speak to M. Le Grand to discuss ways in which we could help CTG protect itself from problems and save money at the same time.

CTG: Yes, I see. Well, M. Le Grand ....

WALTER BARRY: Could you tell me when I could reach him?

CTG: He's ...., then .... in New York. So it is difficult to give you a time.

WALTER BARRY: Could you ask him to ring me?

CTG: I ...., he's ....

WALTER BARRY: Could I speak to someone else, perhaps?

CTG: Who in particular?

WALTER BARRY: A colleague, for example?

CTG: You are speaking to his Personal Assistant. I can deal with calls for M. Le Grand.

WALTER BARRY: Yes, well … er … yes … could I ring him tomorrow?

CTG: No, ...

.... Listen, let me suggest something. You send us details of your products and services, together with references from other companies and then we'll contact you.

WALTER BARRY: Yes, that's very kind. I have your address.

CTG: Very good, Mr … er … er …

WALTER BARRY: Barry. Walter Barry from LCP in London.

CTG: Right, Mr Barry. We look forward to hearing from you.

WALTER BARRY: Thank you. Goodbye.

CTG: Bye.

3 Listen to the beginning of another conversation. A sales manager from a tools manufacturer is telephoning a car components company.

a) Who does the caller ask to speak to?

b) What is the result?

c) Why is the caller successful / not successful here?

Role play 3

Work in pairs. Student A should refer to File card 7A and Student B should use File card 7B.

Role play 4

Keep to the same A or B. Student A should refer to File card 8A and Student B should turn to File card 8B.

TRANSFER

Think about any of the following – whichever is most likely for you now or in the future. Prepare the call (maximum three minutes preparation!). Explain the details of the situation to a colleague or to your teacher, then practise the call.

1 Ring a company to ask for product details or prices.

2 Ring a hotel to book a night's accommodation.

3 Ring a travel agent to ask about flights to a city you need to visit.

If possible record your conversation.

Language Checklist

Telephoning (1)

Introducing yourself
Good morning, Aristo.
Hello, this is … from …
Hello, my name's … calling from …

Saying who you want
I'd like to speak to … , please.
Could I have the … Department, please?
Is … there, please?

Saying someone is not available
I'm sorry he / she's not available …
Sorry, he / she's away / not in / in a meeting / in Milan.

Leaving and taking messages
Could you give him / her a message?
Can I leave him / her a message?

Please tell him / her …
Please ask him / her to ring me on …

Can I take a message?
Would you like to leave a message?
If you give me your number I'll ask him / her to call you later.

Offering to help in other ways
Can anyone else help you?
Can I help you perhaps?
Would you like to speak to his assistant?
Shall I ask him to call you back?

Asking for repetition
Sorry, I didn't catch (your name / your number / your company name / etc.).
Sorry, could you repeat your (name, number, etc.)?
Sorry, I didn't hear that.
Sorry, I didn't understand that.
Could you spell (that / your name), please?

Acknowledging repetition
Okay, I've got that now.
(Mr Kyoto.) I understand.
I see, thank you.

Skills Checklist

Telephoning: Preparation for a call

Reading – background information
Desk preparation
Have the following available:
- relevant documentation / notes
- correspondence or email received
- computer files on screen
- pen and paper
- diary.

Check time available
How much time do you need?
How much time do you have?

Objectives
Who do you want to speak to?
In case of non-availability, have an alternative strategy:
- call back / be called back – when?
- leave a message
- speak to someone else
- write or fax information
- use email.

Do you want to:
- find out information?
- give information?

Introduction
Do you need to refer to:
- a previous call?
- a letter, order, invoice or email?
- someone else (who?)
- an event (what? when?)

Prediction
What do you expect the other person to say / ask you? How will you respond?

Language
Key phrases (see Language Checklist)
Pronunciation
Spelling

Quick Communication Check

1 Introducing yourself and saying what you want

You are on the phone. Complete the sentences with the correct words on the right.

a) Can I ________ to Mr Johnson, please? — speak / say
b) ________ Jan Van der Saar. — My name's / I'm
c) I'm ________ from Amsterdam. — living / calling
d) Can you ________ me the Purchasing Department, please. — fix / give
e) I'd like some ________, please. — informations / informations

2 Leaving and taking messages

Complete the exchanges below with words from the box.

A Can I ________ a message?
B Yes, please. Please ________ him I'll arrive at about three in the afternoon.

C He isn't here at the moment. ________ you like to leave a message?
D Yes, ________ you say Mr Sorensen called?
C I'm sorry, can you ________ your name?
D Yes, it's Sorensen. S … O … R …. E …. N … S … E …. N.

E Shall I ask him to ________ you tomorrow?
F No, it's okay. Please tell him I'll ________ later.

G I'd like to ________ a message for Mr Casey, please.
H Yes, of course. Who's calling?
G Angelo Gherrini, from Milan.

leave
take
could
call
would
tell
ring back
repeat

3 Asking for repetition

Make sentences from the following.

a) can I'm that you repeat sorry? — didn't you I hear.
b) said I'm understand I what didn't you sorry. — you that spell can please?
c) sorry speak I'm slowly more please. — say you what did?

Key

1
a) speak, b) My name's, c) calling, d) give, e) information

2
A take, B tell, C would, D could, C repeat, E call, F ring back, G leave

3
a) I'm sorry, can you repeat that? — I didn't hear you.
b) I'm sorry I didn't understand what you said. — Please can you spell that?
c) I'm sorry, please speak more slowly. — What did you say?

4 Good to hear from you again!

AIMS

- Preparing to make a telephone call
- Receiving calls
- Taking and leaving messages

1 Cross-cultural communication on the telephone (1)

1 **Listen to the three recorded extracts. Match each call to the appropriate picture below. In each case there is a communication problem.**

What is the problem, and how could it be solved?

a

b

c

Conversation 1 Picture ...... Problem ....

Solution ....

Conversation 2 Picture ...... Problem ....

Solution ....

Conversation 3 Picture ...... Problem ....

Solution ....

2 Look briefly at the text. *Before* reading, say:

a) what it is about
b) what the message of the cartoon on the next page is
c) what you think the text probably recommends.

3 Now read the text. Identify the following:

a) something that is important before telephoning
b) advice on how to use your voice
c) advice on checking your understanding
d) examples of 'explicit' cultures – what does this mean?
e) examples of 'subtle' cultures – what does this mean?
f) a possible problem about the phone that you would not have face-to-face.

Telephoning across cultures

Many people are not very confident about using the telephone in English. However, good preparation can make telephoning much easier and more effective. Then, once the call begins, speak slowly and clearly and use simple language.

Check that you understand what has been said. Repeat the most important information, look for confirmation. Ask for repetition if you think it is necessary.

Remember too that different cultures have different ways of using language. Some speak in a very literal way so it is always quite clear what they mean. Others are more indirect, using hints, suggestions and understatement (for example 'not very good results' = 'absolutely disastrous') to put over their message. North America, Scandinavia, Germany and France are 'explicit' countries, while the British have a reputation for not making clear exactly what they mean. One reason for this seems to be that the British use language in a more abstract way than most Americans and continental Europeans. In Britain there are also conventions of politeness and a tendency to avoid showing one's true feelings. For example if a Dutchman says an idea is 'interesting' he means that it is interesting. If an Englishman says that an idea is 'interesting' you have to deduce from the way he says it whether he means it is a good idea or a bad idea.

Meanwhile, for similar reasons Japanese, Russians and Arabs – 'subtle' countries – sometimes seem vague and devious to the British. If they say an idea is interesting it may be out of politeness.

The opposite of this is that plain speakers can seem rude and dominating to subtle speakers, as Americans can sound to the British – or the British to the Japanese.

The British have a tendency to engage in small talk at the beginning and end of a telephone conversation. Questions about the weather, health, business in general and what one has been doing recently are all part of telephoning, laying a foundation for the true purpose of the call. At the end of the call there may well be various pleasantries, *Nice talking to you, Say hello to the family* (if you have met them) and *Looking forward to seeing you again soon.* A sharp, brief style of talking on the phone may appear unfriendly to a British partner. Not all nationalities are as keen on small talk as the British!

Being aware of these differences can help in understanding people with different cultural traditions. The difficulty on the telephone is that you cannot see the body language to help you.

Adapted from *Faxes, phones and foreigners* by kind permission of British Telecommunications plc.

4 Choose the closest definition of the following words from the text.

1 literal (l.7)
   a) direct and clear   b) full of literary style   c) abstract and complicated

2 understatement (l.8)
   a) kind words   b) less strong way of talking   c) clever speech

3 deduce (l.14)
   a) reduce   b) work out   c) disagree

4 vague (l.17)
   a) unclear   b) unfriendly   c) insincere

5 devious (l.17)
   a) rude   b) dishonest   c) clever

6 pleasantries (l.24)
   a) questions   b) requests   c) polite remarks

2 Setting up appointments

1 Listen to the recording. Two colleagues, Bob and Lara, need to meet because a third colleague, Leon, has resigned. As you listen, write the details of the appointment they make in Bob's diary.

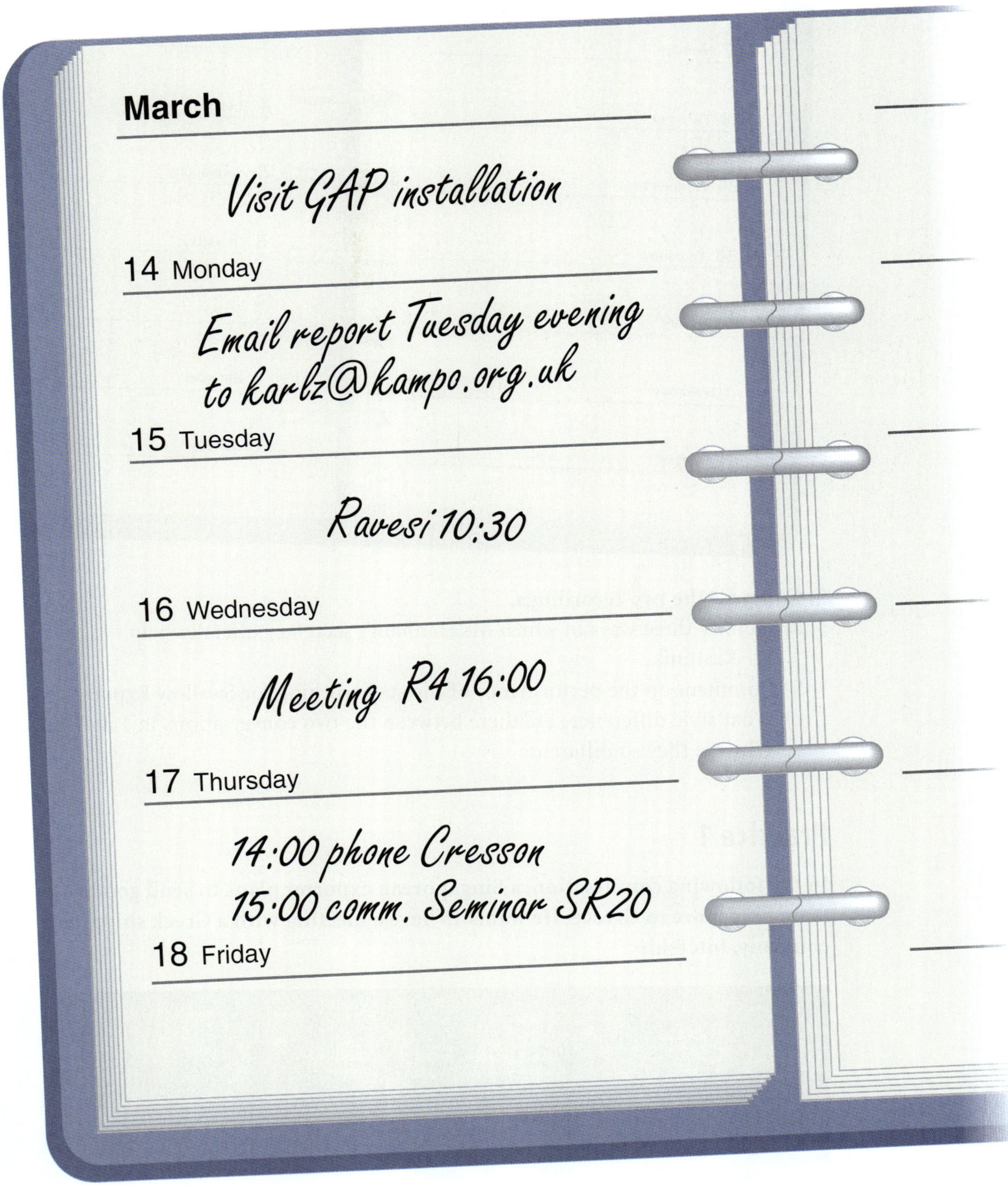

2 **Here Vladimir Kramnik from Moscow calls Joanna Hannam of Swallow Exports Ltd., in London. He wants an appointment with Ms Hannam. Complete the details of the arrangement made in Ms Hannam's diary.**

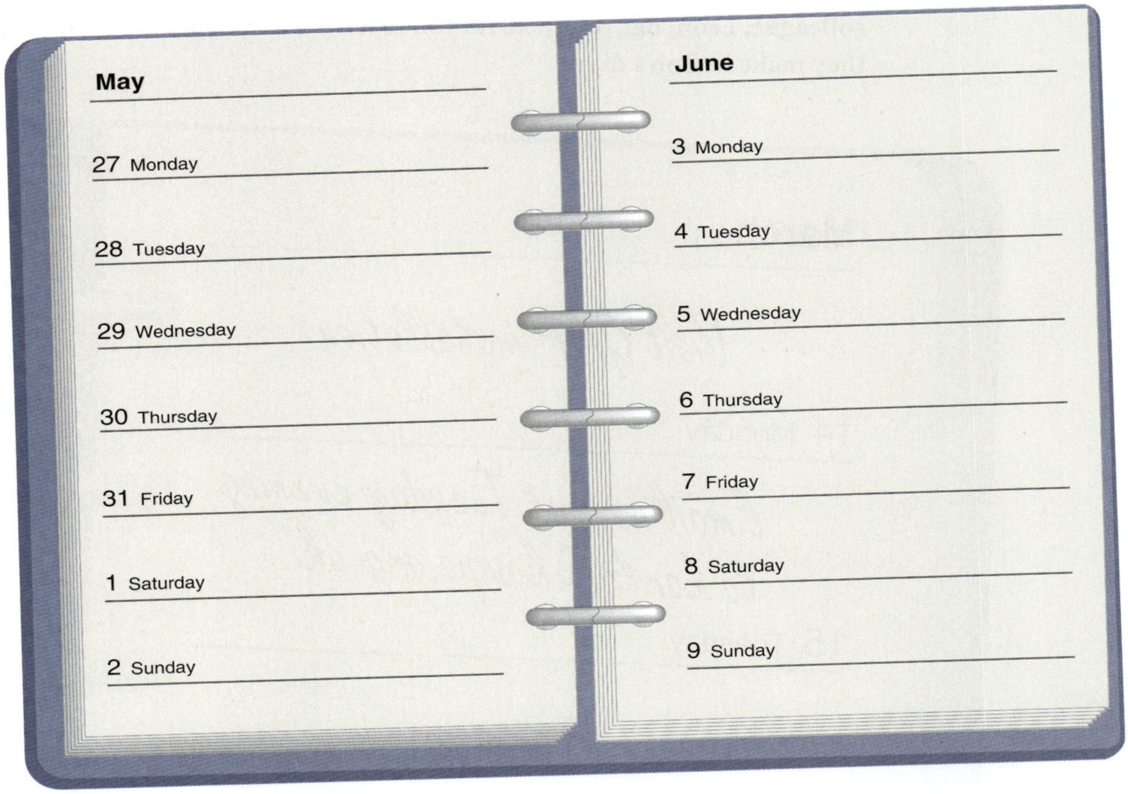

3 **Compare the two recordings.**

a) Identify three ways in which Ms Hannam's secretary offers to help Mr Kramnik.

b) Comment on the performance of the staff working for Swallow Exports.

c) What style differences are there between the two conversations in 1 and 2 above? Why are they so different?

Practice 1

In the following conversation, a Singaporean exporter plans to send goods from Singapore to Greece. He wants to have a meeting with a Greek shipping company, Intership.

Suggest suitable phrases for each step in the conversation, then practise the dialogue with a colleague.

Caller (Computech)	Called Person (Intership)
	'Intership, good morning.'
Greeting.	
Introduce yourself.	
	Check name.
Confirm / correct.	
	Offer to help.
Ask for appointment with Mr Dionis.	
	Ask what it's about.
Explain that you want to discuss transport of goods from Singapore to Athens.	
	Acknowledge – ask when would be a good time.
Suggest next week.	
	Reject – Mr Dionis is away.
	Suggest beginning of next month.
Agree.	
Suggest Monday 3rd.	
	Reject – on Monday Mr Dionis is busy all day.
	Suggest Tuesday.
Agree. Suggest 10.00 a.m.	
	Agree – ask for an email to confirm. Offer to book hotel.
Agree to email. Hotel booking is not necessary.	
Signal end of call.	
	End call / thanks / refer to an email, etc.
End call.	

Now listen to the recording of a model answer.

Practice 2

Sending an email after a telephone conversation is an important way to check that there has been no misunderstanding in the conversation. Many companies also like to have written confirmation of things agreed by telephone.
Use the template below to write an email confirming the arrangements made in the Computech / Intership conversation.

Re: Meeting

From	"P G Smith" pgsmith4@computecharcos.com
To	petakr2@intership.com
Sent	15 April 20–10.45
Subject	Meeting Mr Dionis

Message

3 Changing arrangements

1 **Listen to a conversation between two colleagues, John and Pamela. Note:**
  a) details of the original arrangement
  b) reasons for change
  c) the new arrangement.

2 a) How would you characterise the style of this conversation?
  b) Why is it like that?

3 Listen again to the conversation between John and Pamela. Note the four-part structure of a conversation about changing arrangements. Complete the missing words from the key phrases below:

(1) reference to original appointment

'We're ________ ________ ________ today …'

↓

(2) Statement of problem ⟶ Need for change

'I'm ________, I really can't ________ ________.'

↓

(3) Fixing new appointment

'Can we ________ ________ ________ ________?'

↓

(4) Confirmation

'See you ________ ________.'

Role play 1

Work in pairs. Student A should turn to File card 9A. Student B should use File card 9B.

Role play 2

Keep to the same A or B. Student A should turn to File card 10A. Student B should look at File card 10B.

4 Ending a call

1 **You will hear a recording of Catherine Welsh, a Communications Consultant, talking about telephoning and, in particular, ending phone calls.**

Before you listen, suggest what she might say about the following:

a) ways to avoid misunderstandings
b) a way to check that there's nothing left to say
c) the importance of small talk
d) ways to get off the phone when the other person keeps talking and you are very busy.

2 **Now listen to what Catherine actually says. Compare her suggestions with what you suggested above. Discuss these and other suggestions.**

3 **Hans Rossler is an Export Manager for a German company in Munich. An agent, Hassam Akhtar from Morocco, is planning to visit him. You will hear two versions of how Hans ends a phone conversation with Hassam. Notice how they are different.**

a) What is wrong in the first version?
b) Which key phrase is in the second ending that was not in the first one?

4 **Listen to the next recording of a conversation between two colleagues, Celia Walton and Gerd Hoffmann, who work for a Swiss toy manufacturer.**

a) What is Celia's problem?
b) How does she resolve it?

Practice 3

Sit back-to-back with a colleague and have a telephone conversation about any small talk topic. One of you should try hard to keep the conversation going. The other should politely try to get off the phone.

Reverse roles and repeat the exercise.

TRANSFER 1

Work in pairs, A and B, to devise and practise two role plays. First, each of you should think about your own work or real-life situation. Choose a situation where you need to call someone to arrange a meeting. Explain the situation to your partner. Then practise first one conversation, then the other. Remember to end the call appropriately.

TRANSFER 2

Next time you have to arrange a real meeting by telephone, use the language and recommendations made in this unit. Prepare the call, think about the call structure (see Skills Checklist) and think about how to end the call.

Language Checklist

Telephoning (2)

Stating reason for a call
I'm ringing to …
I'd like to …
I need some information about …

Making arrangements
Could we meet some time next month?
When would be a good time?
Would Thursday at 5 o'clock suit you?
What about July 21st?

That would be fine.
No, sorry, I can't make it then.
Sorry, I'm too busy next week.

Changing arrangements
We've got an appointment for next month, but …
I'm afraid I can't come on that day.
Could we fix an alternative?

Confirming information
So …
Can I check that? You said …
To confirm that …
Can you / Can I confirm that by email?

Ending a call
Right. I think that's all.
Thanks very much for your help.
Do call if you need anything else.
I look forward to … seeing you / your call / your letter / your email / our meeting.
Goodbye and thanks.
Bye for now.

Skills Checklist

Telephoning (2)

Voice
- speed
- clarity
- volume

Structure
- background information
- key information
- repetition, emphasis and confirmation
- possible confirmation by fax

Style
- formal / informal
- cold call / new contact / established contact
- in-company vs customer
  supplier
  outside agent
- colleague / friend / business associate / public
- company image

Structure of a call

Beginning
introduce yourself
get who you want
small talk
state problem / reason for call

Middle
ask questions
get / give information
confirm information

End
signal end
thank other person
small talk
refer to next contact
close call
check that there's nothing else to say

Quick Communication Check

1 Making arrangements

Complete the dialogue below.

A I'd like to (a) v________ you some time next month, to meet Mr Lomas.
B That's (b) f________. I could give you an (c) a________ next week.
A No, unfortunately I'm (d) a________ next week. The (e) f________ week would be okay.
B Yes, well (f) h________ a________ Thursday morning at 10 o'clock?
A That's good. Please can you (g) c________ by email?
B Yes, of course.

2 Changing arrangements

You have an appointment to see Ms Keppel at 11.30 today. Unfortunately your train is delayed. You will not arrive until 12.30. Telephone Ms Keppel's secretary, John Cousins, to explain the problem. Complete the conversation with words from the box.

A Hello, Mr Cousins. This is (your name). I (a) ________ at 11.30, with Ms Keppel. But unfortunately the train (b) ________. I'm going to be (c) ________ .
B I understand. What time do you think you'll arrive?
A About 12.30. Is that a (d) ________ ?
B No, no problem at all.
A Thank you. I am (e) ________ about the (f) ________ .
B It's okay. It's not your fault. See you soon. Thanks for (g) ________ .
A Thank you. Bye for now.

late
delay
have an appointment
problem
sorry
calling
is delayed

3 The structure of a call

Put these sentences in the correct order.

A I understand. That's very kind of you. Thank you very much.
B Can I confirm that? The date is 4 December and it's at the Clyde Hotel.
C Excellent. I look forward to seeing you there.
D I'm ringing to find out some information about the Direct Line Conference in December.
E Hello, my name is Patrick / Patricia Lefèvre. I'm calling from Paris.
F Could you tell me the date and venue of the conference?

1
(a) visit, (b) fine, (c) appointment (d) away, (e) following, (f) how about, (g) confirm
2
(a) have an appointment, (b) is delayed, (c) late, (d) problem, (e) sorry, (f) delay, (g) calling
3
E, D, F, B, A, C

5 Unfortunately there's a problem …

AIMS

- Cross-cultural communication on the telephone (2)
- Problem-solving on the telephone
- Complaints

1 Cross-cultural communication on the telephone (2)

1 **The following text gives some advice about telephoning between different cultures. Before you read it, quickly answer these questions about the organisation of the text:**

a) What is the picture about?
b) How many paragraphs are there?
c) How many main points are probably in the article?

2 **Read the text, then mark the sentences that follow as True (T) or False (F).**

In some countries, like Italy and Britain, conversation is a form of entertainment. There is an endless flow of talk and if you break the flow for a second someone else will pick it up. In other countries there is a higher value placed on listening – it is not only impolite to break in but listeners will consider what has been said in silence before responding. Finland and Japan are examples.

If you are talking to people who are also speaking English as a foreign language, they are likely to leave gaps and silences while they search for words or try to make sense of what you have just said. So be patient and try not to interrupt, as you would hope they would be patient with you.

Every country has its own codes of etiquette. For example it is common for Anglo-Saxons to use first names very quickly, even in a letter or fax or telephone call. Such instant familiarity is much less acceptable in the rest of Europe and Asia where even business partners and colleagues of many years' acquaintance address each other by the equivalent of Mr or Mrs and the last name or job title.

So stick to last names unless you specifically agree to do otherwise. Don't interpret the other person's formality as stiffness or unfriendliness. On the other hand, if business partners with an Anglo-Saxon background get on to first name-terms straight away, don't be surprised.

Above all, one should remember that people do not usually mind if their own codes are broken by foreigners as long as they sense consideration and goodwill. This is much more important than a set of rules of etiquette.

Adapted from *Faxes, phones and foreigners* by kind permission of British Telecommunications plc.

a) For the British and the Italians it is normal to interrupt the other speaker during the conversation. ☐

b) A special importance is attached to listening in Japanese and Finnish cultures. ☐

c) One should interrupt and try to help speakers who may have difficulty in saying what they want to say. ☐

d) It is unusual for Americans and British to use first names early in a business relationship. ☐

e) It doesn't matter if you break certain social rules if it is clear that you are sensitive to other people. ☐

f) Etiquette is the critical point in telephoning between different cultures. ☐

3 Which do you think is the most important point?

2 Problem-solving on the telephone

1 Lee Santana is a telecommunications equipment retailer from Los Angeles. Listen to the recording of a conversation he has with a supplier, Yoshinaga Takafumi. He works for AKA Company, a Japanese telephone systems manufacturer.

a) Identify the problem and the suggested solution.

b) Listen again. Do you think Yoshinaga Takafumi provided good customer service? If so, how?

c) Notice how the conversation follows the structure shown here:

Customer	Supplier
Introduction and getting who you want. →	Greeting and small talk.
Small talk. ←	
Stating problem. →	Apology.
	Suggesting solution.
Agreeing to suggested solution. ←	
Confirmation. →	Apology.
End call. ←	End call.

Practice 1

Work in pairs, A and B. Create a dialogue based on the prompts below. A is the Client Services Manager of Keene Investments who calls B, a financial adviser. A is B's boss.

Eric / Erica King (A)	Charles / Charlotte Heppel (B)
	Answer the phone.
Introduce yourself and say there's a problem. →	Respond – ask what?
Respond – explain problem: A client – Sandra Henson – has phoned. She expected CH to visit yesterday. No one came. →	Respond – the client has made a mistake. The appointment is for *next* week.
Respond appropriately. Ask CH if he / she wrote with details of the visit. →	Yes. Offer to call Sandra Henson.
End call (small talk). →	End call.

Now listen to a recording of a model answer.

3 Complaints

1 **Hamid Nadimi of Ahmed Al-Hamid & Co. in Riyadh telephones Peter Carr, from Stella Communications plc, Birmingham, with a complaint.**

a) Listen and identify the problem.

b) Listen again and write the remaining key information on the flow chart:

Problem?

Mr Nadimi complains that

....

↓

Response?

Mr Carr says ....

....

↓

Action decided?

Mr Carr promises ....

Discuss how Peter Carr handles the call. Do you think he said the right things?

2 **Work in pairs to create a new version of the above conversation beginning with the same basic problem. Provide better customer service in your version.**

3 **Imagine you are Peter Carr. Following the above phone call and then a conversation with Mr Bains, write an email to Mr Nadimi. Tell him Mr Bains will return in four days with the parts and the system will be repaired within five days. Use the email outline template below:**

STELLA COMMUNICATIONS

TO hamidnadimi@ahmedalhamid.com (Hamid Nadimi)

FROM p.carr@stella.birmingham.co.uk

SUBJECT **Faulty Valves on Pipeline System**

Following our .... I am pleased to tell you that Mr Bains .... in four days and .... within five days.

If there is any way that I can be of further assistance please do not .... me again.

Also, let me assure you of .... in future.

Best regards

Peter Carr

Customer Services

Practice 2

Suggest what the person complaining and the person handling the complaint could say in the following situations. Then listen to the recordings of model answers.

1 A printer purchased three months ago has broken down for a fourth time.

2 An order from a hospital for 500 × 100 ml of medicated gel has not arrived.

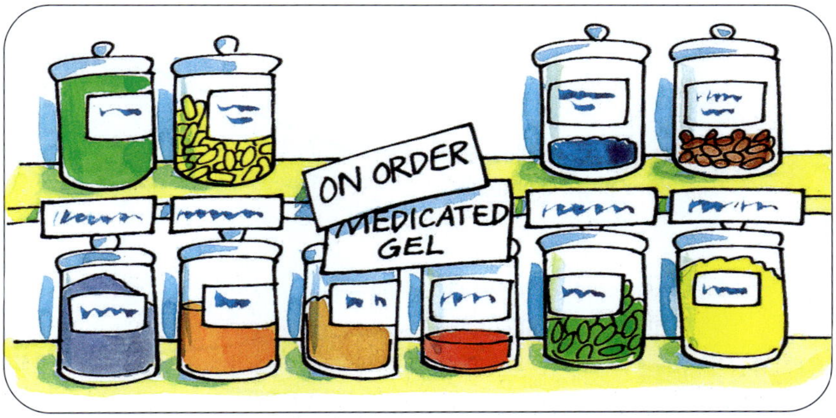

3 A travel agent promised to send out an airline ticket for departure tomorrow. It has not arrived.

Practice 3

Use the flow chart below as the basis for a telephone conversation involving a complaint.

Berraondo S.A.	Tao Loon Company (Sales Office)
	Answer.
Greeting. Introduce yourself.	
	Offer to help.
Explain problem. Order HF5618 for 20 printers. Only 17 have arrived.	
	Express surprise.
This is second time you have received an incomplete delivery.	
	Suggest possible error in order administration.
Agree – say you need the other three printers urgently.	
Delays are costing you goodwill – unhappy customers.	
	Explain stock problems.
Ask for a promise of delivery date – ASAP.	
	Promise next Monday.
Complain – you want despatch now.	
	Express regret – not possible.
Ask for an email to confirm despatch.	
	Agree – apologise.
	End call.

Now listen to the recording of a model answer.

Role play

Work in pairs, A and B. Student A should look at File card 11A and Student B should look at File card 11B.

TRANSFER 1

Think of examples of where you have needed to resolve a problem on the telephone, perhaps with a colleague (an internal problem) or with another company (an external problem).
Did the problem involve a complaint?
Say what the situation was and what problem occurred.
Explain any difficulty you had and say how the problem was resolved.

TRANSFER 2

Prepare a conversation typical of the sorts of problems or complaints you are faced with in your working life. Explain the situation and the roles involved to a colleague and then perform the conversation.

Language Checklist

Telephoning (3)

Stating reason for the call
I'm ringing about ...
Unfortunately, there's a problem with ...
I'm ringing to complain about ...

Explaining the problem
There seems to be ...
We haven't received ...
The ... doesn't work.
The quality of the work is below standard.
The specifications are not in accordance with our order.

Referring to previous problems
It's not the first time we've had this problem.
This is the (third) time this has happened.
Three months ago ...
We had a meeting about this and you assured us that ...

Threatening
If the problem is not resolved ...
we'll have to reconsider our position.
we'll have to renegotiate the contract.
we'll contact other suppliers.
the consequences could be very serious.

Handling complaints and other problems

Asking for details
Could you tell me exactly what ... ?
Can you tell me ... ?
What's the ... ?

Apologising
I'm sorry to hear that.
I'm very sorry about the problem / delay / mistake ...

Denying an accusation
No, I don't think that can be right.
I'm sorry but I think you're mistaken.
I'm afraid that's not quite right.
I'm afraid that can't be true.

Skills Checklist

Telephoning (3)

If you receive a complaint:
- consider your company's reputation
- express surprise
- ask for details
- suggest action
- promise to investigate
- make reasonable suggestions, offers to help.

Consider your customer and:
- show polite understanding
- use active listening
- reassure customer.

If you make a complaint:
- prepare for the call
- be sure of the facts
- have documentation available
- decide what you require to resolve the problem – at least partially – or completely.

Who is to blame?
Who is responsible?
Are you talking to the right person?
Was your order or your specifications correct?
Were you partly responsible for arrangements which went wrong, e.g. transport?
Does responsibility actually lie elsewhere, i.e. with a third party?

If you do not get what you want:
- keep control – state what you need calmly
- do you need to continue to do business with the other side?
- if you do, keep a good relationship
- express disappointment – not anger
- don't use threats – unless you have to!

Quick Communication Check

1 Saying why you are calling

Match the phrase on the left with the correct ending.

1 The reason for my call …	a) advice on …
2 I'm ringing about…	b) something about your services?
3 I need to talk to	c) a supply problem.
4 I would like some	d) is a technical matter.
5 Can you tell me	e) someone about …

2 Explaining the problem

Replace the underlined words with words in the box which mean the same.

1 We are still waiting for the goods to arrive.
2 There seems to be something wrong with the machine.
3 The power switch is broken.
4 We still have not received an answer to our letter.
5 I don't understand why we have not received the money you owe us.
6 I don't understand how to operate the machine.

> please explain
> delivery
> not working
> a problem
> a reply
> the instructions
> payment

3 Handling complaints

Complete the exchanges below with words from the box.

> you back reference
> serial number
> delivery transfer
> delay comes back
> hold ask him
> sorry available

A There seems to be a problem with the machine.
B I'm (a) .... to hear that.
Do you have a customer (b) .... number?
What's the (c) .... on the machine?
C I'd like to speak to Mr Davis.
D He's not (d) .... at the moment but I'll
(e) .... to call (f) .... as soon as he (g) ....
E I think there's a problem with the invoice.
F If you (h) .... on, I'll (i) .... you to the right department.
G We still haven't received the goods.
H I'm sorry. We've had a (j) .... in distribution.
Everything should be okay for a (k) .... next week.

Key
1
1 d), 2 c), 3 e) 4 a), 5 b)
2
1 delivery, 2 a problem, 3 not working, 4 a reply,
5 Please explain, payment, 6 the instructions
3
(a) sorry, (b) reference, (c) serial number,
(d) available, (e) ask him, (f) you back, (g) comes
back, (h) hold, (i) transfer, (j) delay, (k) delivery

MODULE 3

PRESENTATIONS

6 Planning and getting started

AIMS

- Presentation technique and preparation
- The audience
- Structure (1) The introduction

1 Presentation technique and preparation

1 Look at the picture. What kind of situation is this? Do you think the presenter looks as if she is giving a good presentation? Why? Why not?

Discuss or make notes on the characteristics of a good presentation. Think about both the *content* and the *way* the speaker presents information.

2 The text below contains several recommendations for giving effective presentations. Scan the text to match the seven points below to the right paragraph, a–g. You do not have to read the text in detail.

1 Choose visuals to support the presentation. ☐
2 Have a simple, clear structure. ☐
3 Show enthusiasm. ☐
4 Use PowerPoint. ☐
5 Making informal presentations. ☐
6 Consider the audience. ☐
7 Dealing with nerves. ☐

What advice from Luis E. Lamela do *you* think is the most important?

a The key to a successful oral presentation is to keep things simple. I try to stick to three points. I give an overview of the points, present them to the audience, and summarize them at the end.

b My purpose or desired outcome, the type of audience, and the message dictate the formality of the presentation, the kind of visuals, the number of anecdotes, and the jokes or examples that I use. Most of my presentations are designed to sell, to explain, or to motivate. When I plan the presentation, I think about the audience. Are they professionals or nonprofessionals? Purchasers or sellers? Providers or users? Internal or external? My purpose and the audience mix determine the tone and focus of the presentation.

c When I make a presentation, I use the visuals as the outline. I will not use notes. I like to select the kind of visual that not only best supports the message but also best fits the audience and the physical location. PowerPoint, slides, overhead transparencies, and flip charts are the four main kinds of visuals I use.

d PowerPoint and slide presentations work well when I am selling a product or an idea to large groups (15 people or more). In this format, I like to use examples and graphs and tables to support my message in a general way.

e In small presentations, including one-on-ones and presentations where the audience is part of the actual process, I like transparencies or flip charts. They allow me to be more informal.

f I get very, very nervous when I speak in public. I handle my nervousness by just trying to look as if, instead of talking to so many people, I'm walking in and talking to a single person. I don't like to speak behind lecterns. Instead, I like to get out and just be open and portray that openness: 'I'm here to tell you a story.'

g I try very hard for people to enjoy my presentations by showing enthusiasm on the subject and by being sincere. I try not to use a hard sell – I just try to report or to explain – and I think that comes across. In addition, it helps that I am speaking about something that I very strongly believe in and something that I really, really enjoy doing.

Luis E. Lamela, February 11, 1997
From *Business and Administrative Communication* by Kitty Locker, Irwin McGraw-Hill, 1998.

3 What are the key considerations involved in *preparing* a presentation?

4 Listen to a group of management trainees talking about the preparation of presentations. They mention eight key areas, each represented by one of the pictures below. Number the pictures in the order in which they are mentioned.

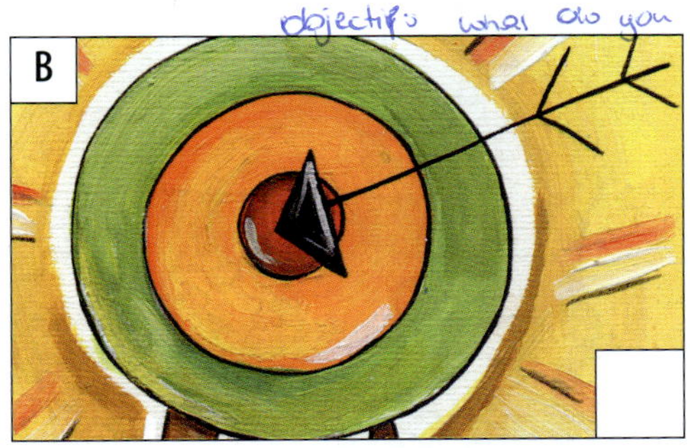

Discussion

Comment on any of the points mentioned in the discussion you have heard. Which do you think are the most important? Do you feel it is necessary to write out a presentation?

2 The audience

1 **Read the comments from the audience who are listening to a presentation at an international conference. What caused the problem in each case?**

a) 'What on earth is he talking about?'~'I've no idea!'
b) 'Hey, Sarah! Wake up! He's finished!'
c) 'Read that! I can't read that! I'd need a pair of binoculars!'
d) 'Speak up! I can't hear a thing!'
e) 'Summarise four main points? I only noticed one! Have I been asleep?'

2 **Look at the following situations.**

A medical conference in Tokyo with papers on new techniques in open-heart surgery.

The Purchasing and Product Managers of a Taiwanese company interested in buying some production equipment from your company.

An internal meeting of administrative staff to discuss a new accounting procedure.

A staff meeting to discuss a charity event for earthquake victims.

Imagine you have to give a brief presentation in two of the above situations, plus one other situation that you decide. Make brief notes on the following:

a) Will your talk be formal or informal?
b) What are the audience's expectations in terms of technical detail, expertise, etc.?
c) What is the audience's probable level of specialist knowledge? Are they experts or non-experts?
d) How long will your talk be: five minutes, 20 minutes, half a day, or longer?
e) What is your policy on questions? Will the audience interrupt or will they ask questions afterwards? Will there be any discussion?
f) How will you help the audience to remember what you tell them?

3 Structure (1) The introduction

1 **In any presentation the beginning is crucial. Certainly some things are essential in an introduction and others are useful. Here is a list of what could be included in an introduction. Mark them according to how necessary they are using the following scale:**

Essential		Useful		Not necessary
1	2	3	4	5

Subject / Title of talk. ☐
Introduction to oneself, job title, etc. ☐
Reference to questions and / or discussion. ☐
Reference to the programme for the day. ☐
Reference to how long you are going to speak for. ☐
Reference to using PowerPoint. ☐
The scope of your talk: what is and is not included. ☐
An outline of the structure of your talk. ☐
A summary of the conclusions. ☐

2 **Listen to the beginning of a presentation on the marketing plans for a new telecommunications system produced by Telco.**

a) Is it a good introduction?
b) Why? Why not?
c) Label the structure of the talk.

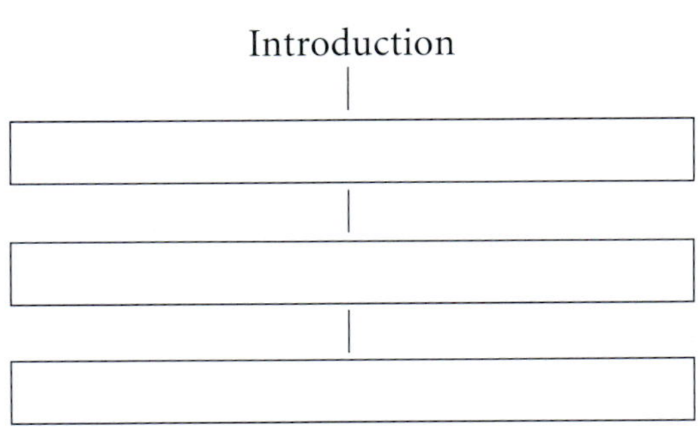

3 Now listen to a second example of an introduction to a presentation. This one is about plans to develop a new production plant in Taiwan.

As you listen, think about these points:

a) Is it a good introduction?
b) Why? Why not?
c) Label the structure of the talk.

Introduction

i)
ii)

End / Discussion

4 Work in pairs. Each of you should suggest a possible phrase for each of the prompts below.

a) Greet your audience.
b) Introduce yourself.
c) Give the title of your talk.
d) Describe the structure of your talk.
e) Explain that the audience can interrupt if they want.
f) Say something about the length of your talk.
g) Say a colleague will be showing a video later.

Now listen to the recording of a model introduction based on suitable phrases for a–g.

Practice 1

Use the notes below to prepare a brief introduction to a talk on safety for a manufacturing company.

New safety conditions for production staff

1 Protective clothing

2 Training in accident prevention

3 Changes to working practices

Questions / Discussion

Listen to the recording of a model answer after you have given your own version.

Practice 2

Give a one-minute introduction only to a talk on any topic you like! If you cannot think of a topic, choose from the list below:

your home town	your favourite sport	tourism
your first-ever job	eating out	holidays
a thing you really like	your previous job	your hobbies

TRANSFER

Prepare an introduction to a short talk on one of the following:

- your company and / or its products / services
- any company you know well
- an institution that you know well.

Decide who the audience is. Make notes. Look at the Skills Checklist on page 62 and remember in particular to consider the points under the heading *Audience*. Look at the Language Checklist on page 62.

Do not write the whole text. When you are ready, practise your introduction. If you can, make a recording. When you have finished, answer the following questions:

- Did you make a recording? If you did, listen to it now.
- Does the recording sound well prepared and competent?
- Did you read everything you said from detailed notes?
- Did you talk using only brief notes?
- Did you speak clearly and not too fast?
- Did you outline the topic, structure and content of your talk?
- Did you refer to audience questions and to discussion?
- How could you improve your introduction?

Language Checklist

The introduction to a presentation

Greeting
Good morning / afternoon ladies and gentlemen.
(Ladies and) Gentlemen ...
Hello, everyone.

Subject
I plan to say a few words about ...
I'm going to talk about ...
The subject of my talk is ...
The theme of my presentation is ...
I'd like to give you an overview of ...

Structure
I've divided my talk into (three) parts.
My talk will be in (three) parts.
I'm going to divide ...
First ...
Second ...
Third ...
In the first part ...
Then in the second part ...
Finally ...

Timing
My talk will take about ten minutes.
The presentation will take about two hours ... but there'll be a twenty-minute break in the middle.
We'll stop for lunch at 12 o'clock.

Policy on questions / discussion
Please interrupt if you have any questions.
After my talk there'll be time for a discussion and any questions.

Skills Checklist

Effective presentations – planning and preparation

Audience
- expectations
- technical knowledge
- size
- questions and / or discussion

Speaker's competence
- knowledge
- presentation technique

Content
- what to include
- length / depth (technical detail)
- number of key ideas

Structure
- sequence
  - beginning, middle, end
- repetition, summarising

Delivery
- style
  - formal / informal
  - enthusiasm / confidence
- voice
  - variety / speed
  - pauses
- body language
  - eye contact
  - gesture / movement
  - posture

Visual aids
- PowerPoint
- type / design / clarity
- relevance

Practice
- tape recorder
- script or notes

Room
- size / seating
- equipment (does it work?)
- sound quality

Language
- simple / clear
- spelling
- sentence length
- structure signals

Quick Communication Check

1 Subject

Complete the spaces in the five opening sentences of presentations.

1 My t.................... today is about our plans for entering new markets.

2 I'd l.................... to say something today about the AX project.

3 The presentation will give you an o.................... of our organisation.

4 The t.................... of my talk is the 'Single European Market and Competition Policy'.

5 This morning I want to e.................... the special relationship between us and our suppliers.

2 Presentation structure

The classic presentation has three parts. Here are six sentences from the introduction to a presentation. Put them in the right order.

a) I'm going to talk about the new organisation of our European Sales. ☐
b) Afterwards you can ask any questions or say what you think. ☐
c) Good afternoon, everyone. My presentation today is about changes in our organisation. ☐
d) Finally I'll describe the new arrangement – the new system. ☐
e) First I'll describe the current situation – how things are now. ☐
f) Then I'll explain why we have to change this. ☐

3 Introducing your presentation

Make verb + noun phrases by matching the verbs below to the right words. See the example.

1 to talk about	*e*	a) questions
2 to explain	......	b) an overview
3 to say	......	c) a few words
4 to give	......	d) the problem
5 to divide	......	e) something
6 to answer	......	f) the talk into x parts

4 Your policy on questions and discussion

Make sentences from the words below.

1 like whenever interrupt you
2 if questions have ask you please any
3 questions until save any the please end
4 you have I a for handout
5 points handout my the includes main the of talk
6 few may notes take to want you a
7 be will discussion there a later

1
1 talk, 2 like, 3 overview, 4 title, 5 explain
2
a) 2, b) 6, c) 1, d) 5, e) 3, f) 4
3
1e), 2d), 3c), 4b), 5f), 6a)
4
1 Interrupt whenever you like.
2 Please ask if you have any questions.
3 Please save any questions until the end.
4 I have a handout for you.
5 The handout includes the main points of my talk.
6 You may want to take a few notes.
7 There will be a discussion later.

7 Image, impact and making an impression

AIMS

- Using visual aids: general principles
- Talking about the content of visual aids
- Describing change

1 Using visual aids: general principles

1 **What points do the illustrations imply?**

2 Look at the pictures below. Label the tools used to present visual information.

3 Comment on how visual information is being presented in these pictures, then produce five key recommendations for how to use visual supports in a presentation.

4 Read the text below and find:

a) eight advantages of using visual aids

b) three warnings about using visual aids.

Dinckel and Parnham (1985) say that 'The great danger (in using visual aids) is that presenters place the major emphasis on visual aids and relegate themselves to the minor role of narrator or technician. You are central to the presentation. The visual aid needs you, your interpretation, your explanation, your conviction and your justification.' Visual aids can make information more memorable and they help the speaker. However, they must literally support what the speaker says and not simply replace the spoken information. It is also not enough to just read text from a visual aid.

There are many advantages to the correct use of visual aids. They can show information which is not easily expressed in words or they can highlight information. They cause the audience to employ another sense to receive information, they bring variety and therefore increase the audience's attention. They save time and they clarify complex information.

Adapted from Bernice Hurst, *The Handbook of Communication Skills* (London: Kogan Page, 1991).

2 Talking about the content of visual aids

1 Label the following using words from the boxes.

pie chart map bar graph table diagram picture line graph flow chart plan

a

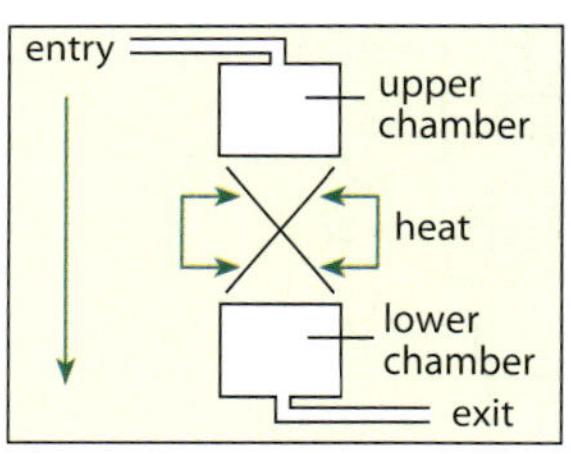

b

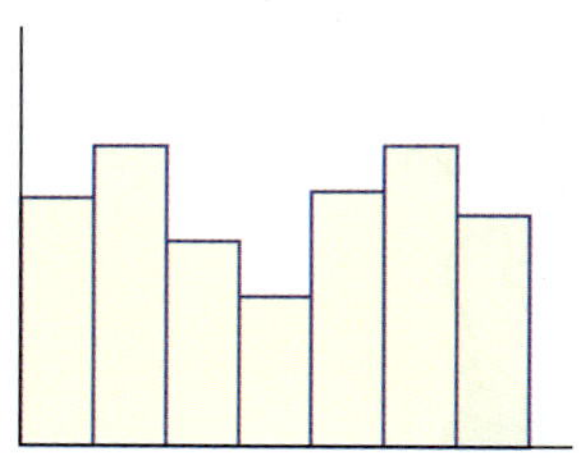

c

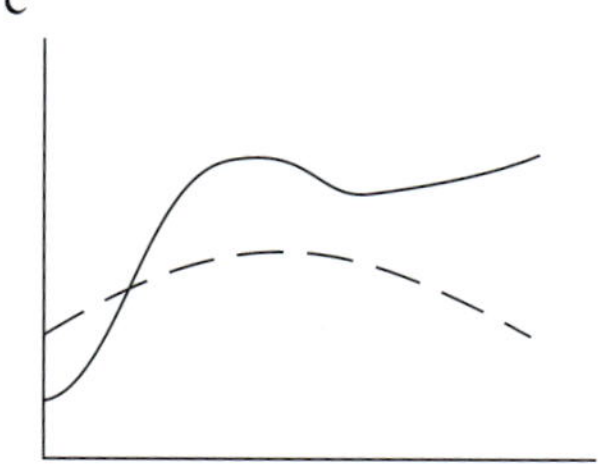

d

e

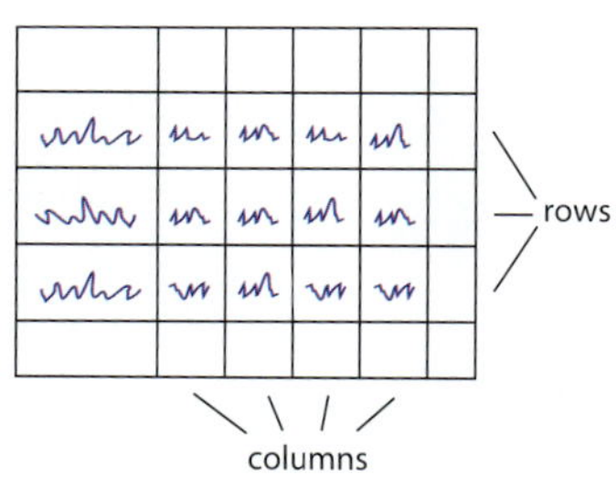

f

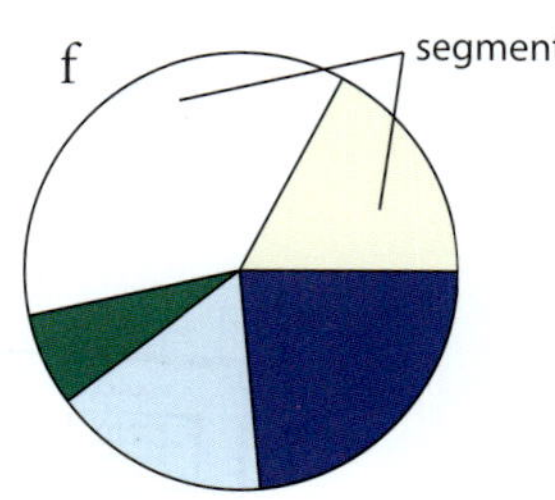

g

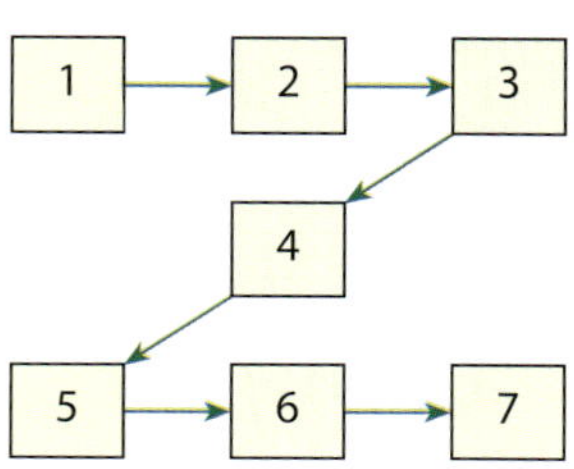

h

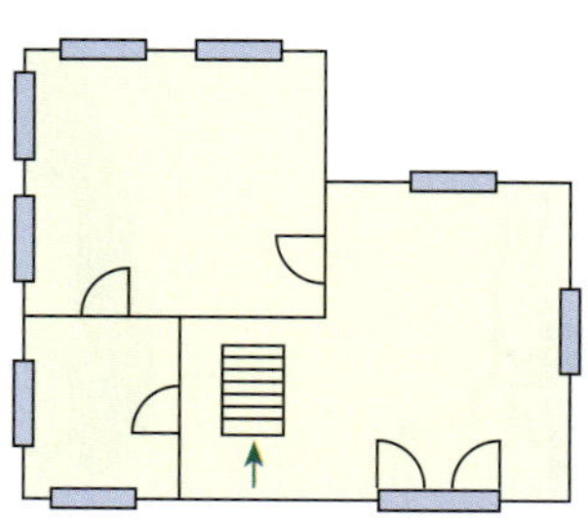

i

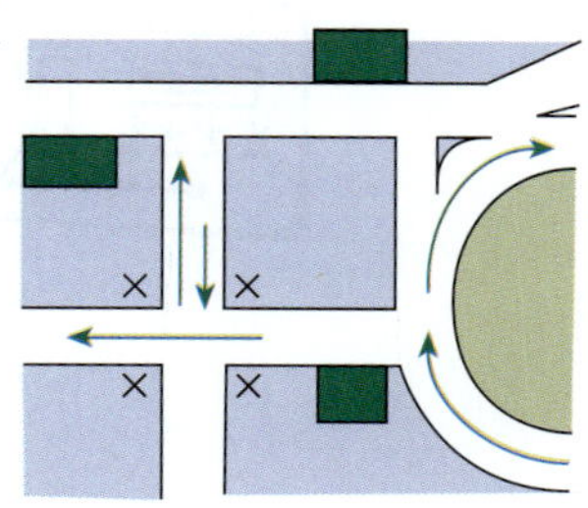

dotted line   curve   fluctuating line   vertical axis
broken line   undulating line   horizontal axis   solid line

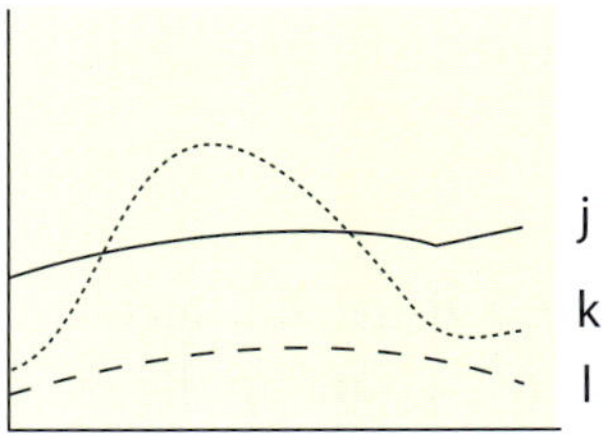

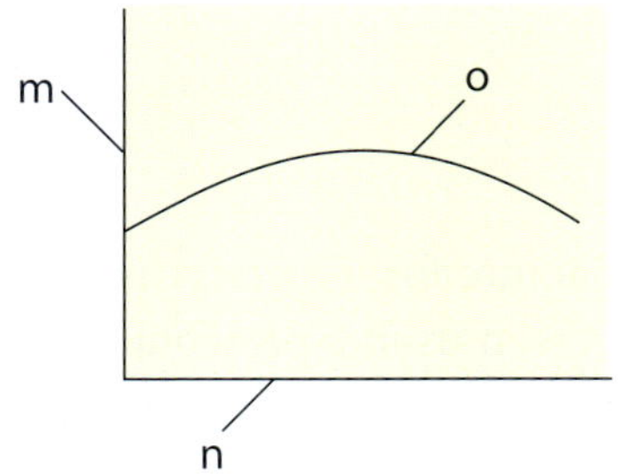

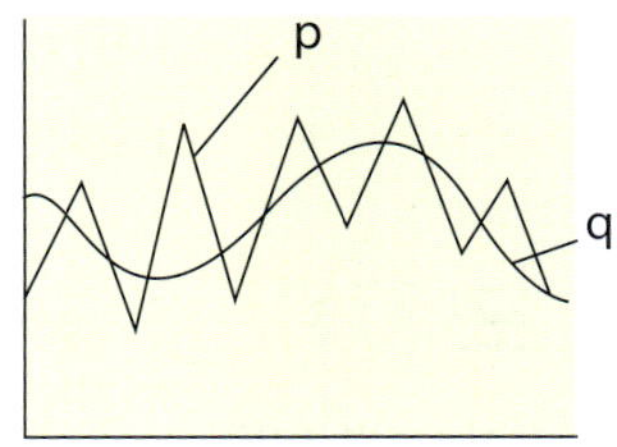

2 A project manager for FDF, a manufacturing company, makes a presentation on the reasons for choosing a particular location for a new plant. Listen to four extracts from his talk.

a) Match each extract (1–4) to the correct diagram below.

a

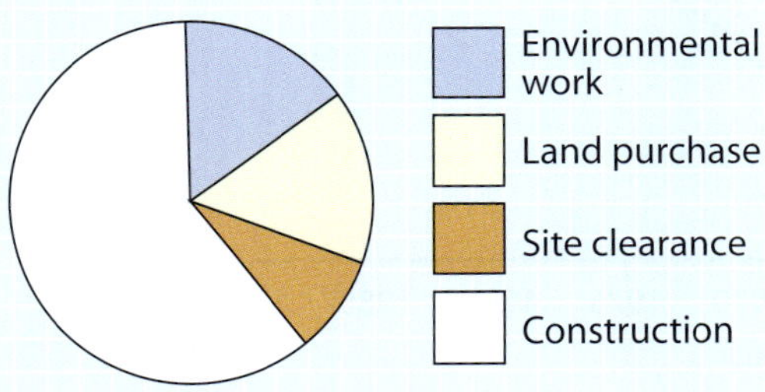

b

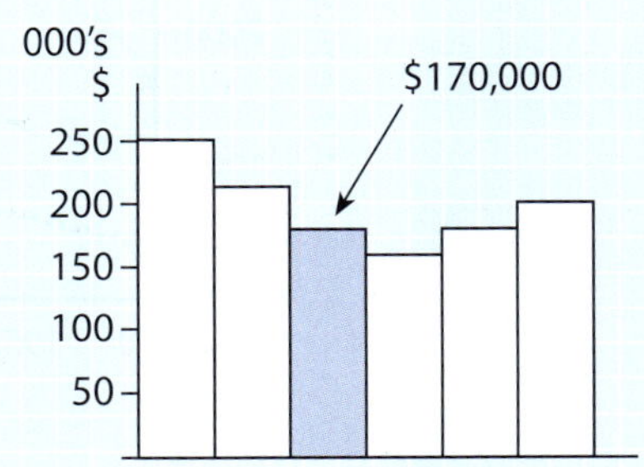

c

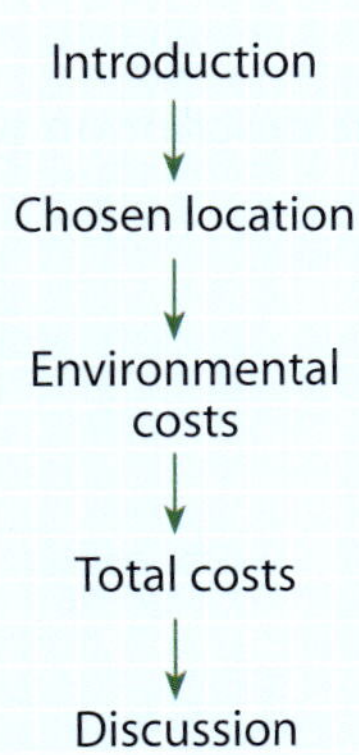

d

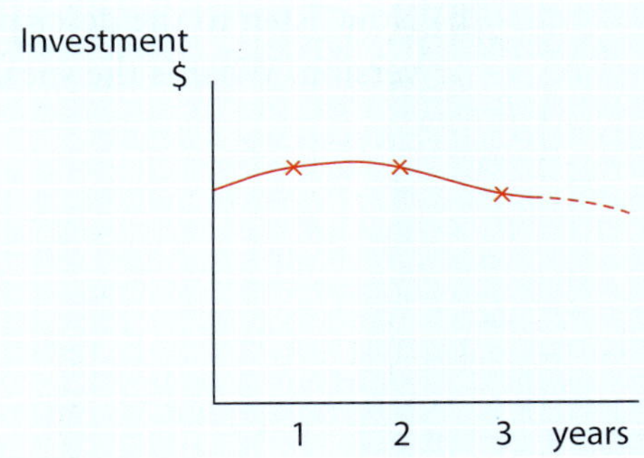

b) Listen again. What is the key point the speaker makes about each picture?

Extract 1: ....

Extract 2: ....

Extract 3: ....

Extract 4: ....

3 a) Suggest a typical structure for how a speaker could describe a visual aid, such as the graph below, taken from a presentation, 'World energy – going up the chimney', given at an environment conference.

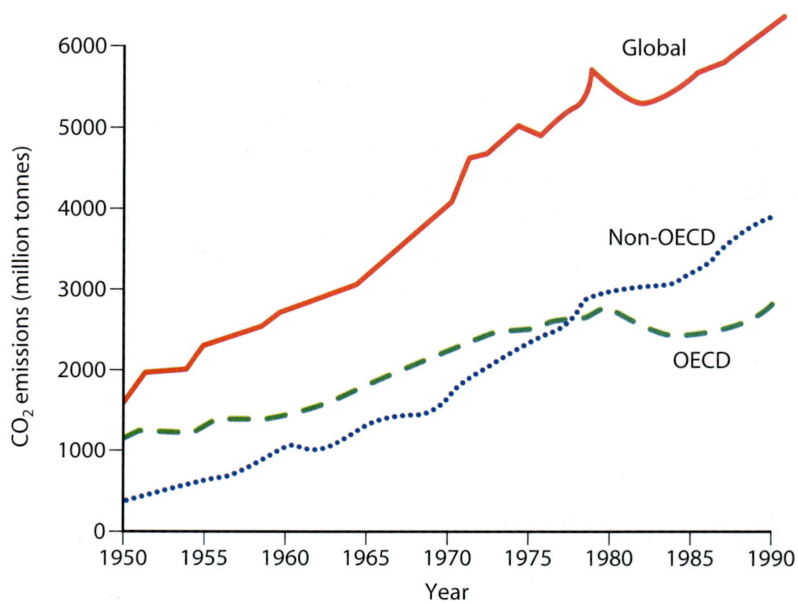

Fig. 1. Trends in CO_2 emissions between 1950 and 1990. OECD (Organisation for Economic Cooperation and Development) countries (developed world) compared with non-OECD countries

b) Now listen to the description on the tape. Compare the description with your own version. What is the speaker's main point?

c) Listen again. Complete the spaces in the following sentences.

1 Now, I'd like (a) .... this graph. It (b) .... the (c) ....
in CO_2 emissions between 1950 and 1990.

2 On (d) .... you see the CO_2 emissions in millions of tons, while the
(e) .... time over 40 years. (f) .... the global total at
the top, the broken line here is OECD countries, or developed countries.
The dotted line shows non-OECD, or developing countries.

3 What we (g) .... here is, quite clearly, (h) .... in
CO_2 emissions.

4 In pairs, suggest an explanation for the information below, from the same presentation.

Note: For each picture, select two or three main points for special emphasis in your explanation.

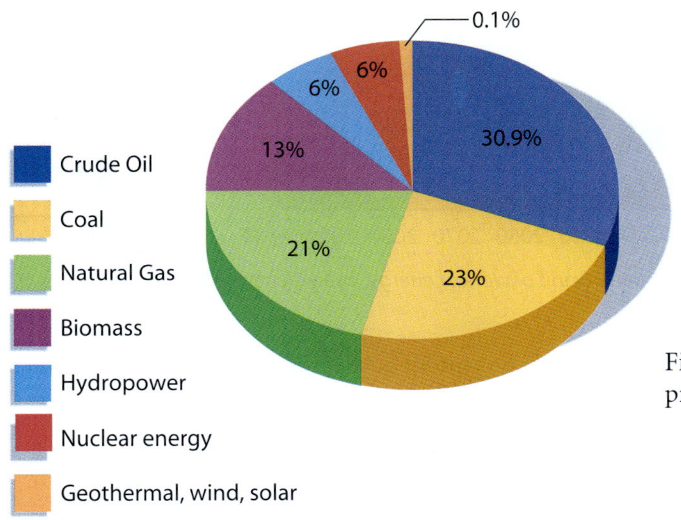

Fig. 2. Sources for energy production

	Nuclear	**Coal, oil and other fossil fuels**	**Hydro, wind and renewable sources**
France	76	9	12
Sweden	46	3	50
Spain	30	49	21
Germany	29	64	8
UK	28	68	4
Netherlands	4	88	8
Denmark	0	89	11
EU Average	34	50	17

Fig. 3. Electricity generation by fuel used: selected EU countries by comparison, 1998.

Now listen to a recording of a model presentation.

Practice 1

Imagine using the graph below in a presentation about air quality. Suggest how you would describe it. Use the prompts a–d.

Fossil Fuel Farewell

Renewable energy could supply all the world's energy needs by the year 2100

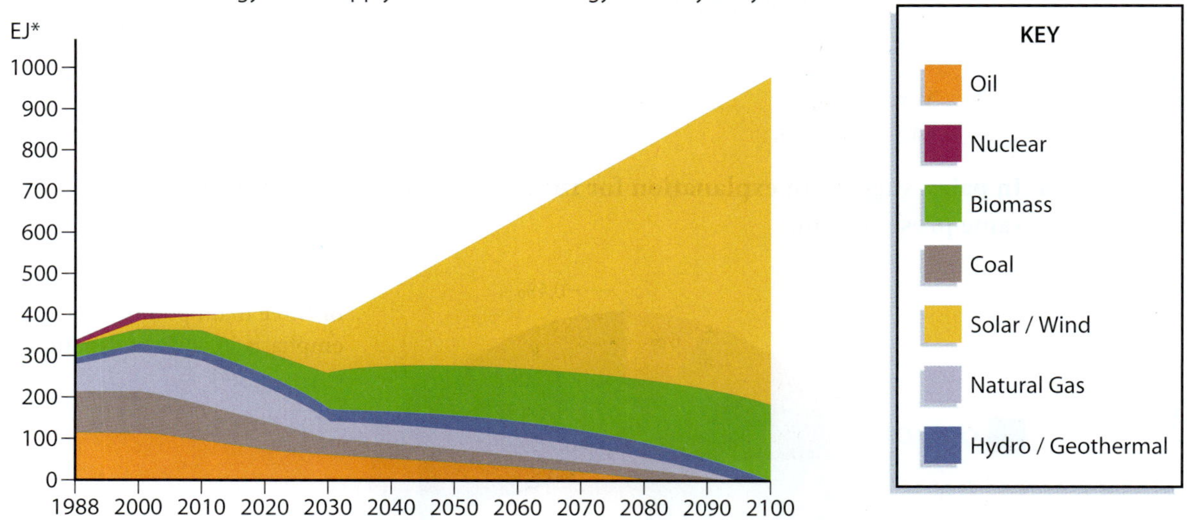

**Exajoules* (1EJ = 10^{18} joules). A joule is a unit of work or energy, equivalent to 0.239 calories.*

Fig. 4. Global vehicle CO_2 emissions assuming no improvements in vehicle efficiency.

a) 'Now ....'

b) 'It shows ....'

c) 'The vertical .... while ....'

d) 'Clearly, we can see that ....'

Now listen to the recording.

3 Describing change

1 **The vocabulary in this section is used to describe movement or trends. This task checks your knowledge of several key words and phrases used to describe movement. For example:**

a

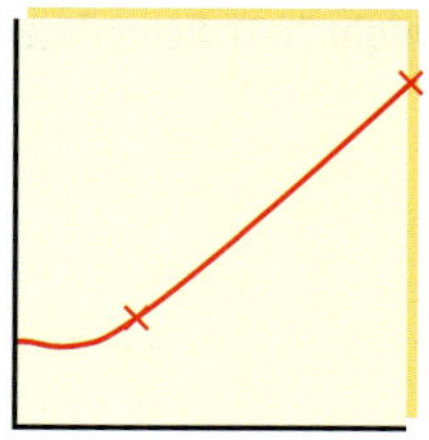

increased rapidly

b

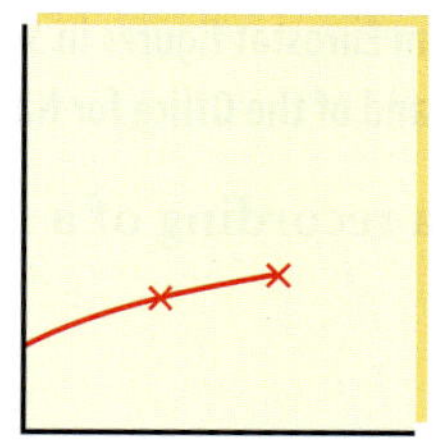

went up a bit

Match the following pictures with the correct phrase:

climbed slightly   increased steadily   dropped markedly
declined a little   rose dramatically

c

d

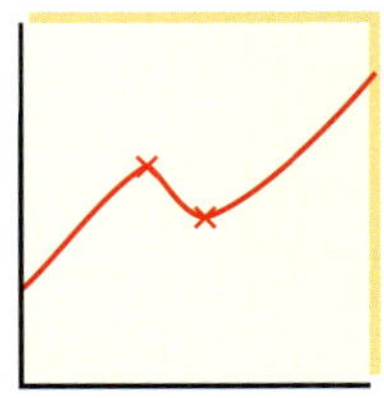

e

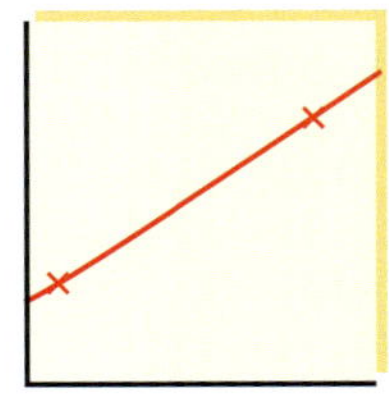

f

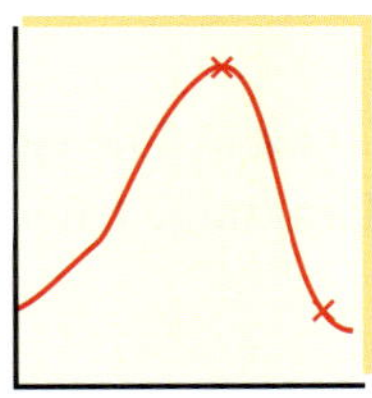

g

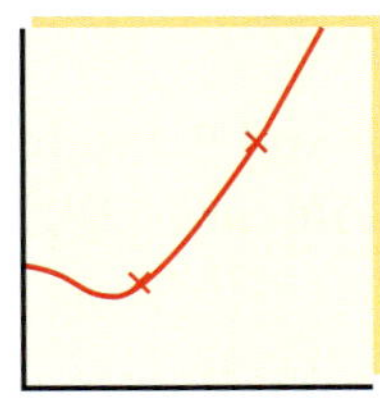

2 Look at the diagrams and write other words to describe what each one shows. Try to find the noun form for each verb, for example *to increase / an increase.*

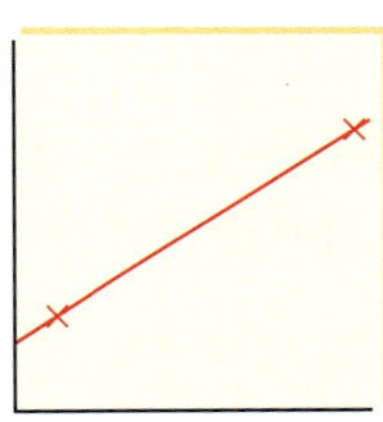

a) to increase   an increase

to ....

to ....

to ....

to ....

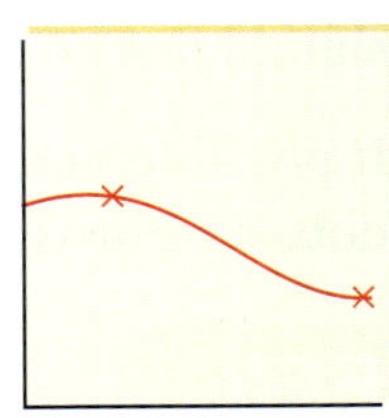

b) to decrease   a decrease

to ....

to ....

to ....

to ....

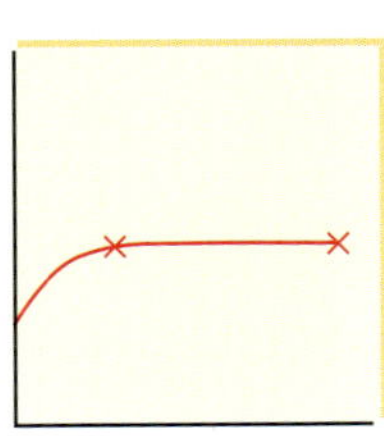

c) to stay the same

to ....

to ....

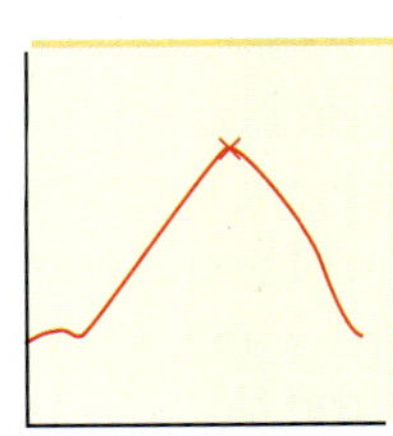

d) to reach a maximum

to ....

to ....

e) to recover a recovery

to ....

to ....

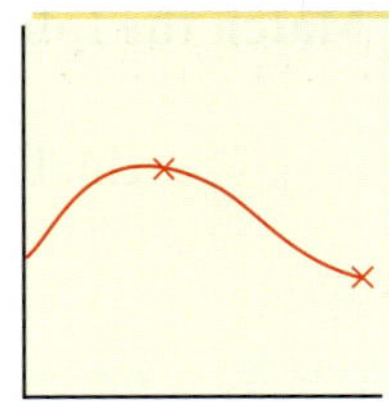

f) to deteriorate a deterioration

to ....

Role play

Work in pairs, A and B. Student A should look at File card 12A and Student B should look at File card 12B. Look at the Language Checklist if you need to.

Practice 2

Draw a line graph for use in a presentation. Choose any situation or subject, real or imagined. If possible draw the picture on an overhead transparency. Then present the graph as you would in a presentation. Your description should last no more than a minute.

If possible, construct a graph that makes comparisons possible. Use solid, dotted or broken lines (or colours) to make the picture clear.

TRANSFER

Think of your professional or study situation. Prepare any pictures or visuals for use in a presentation. Prepare a description for each one.
Record your description without reading directly from your notes, though you may of course look at the pictures.
If you can, video record your presentation of the pictures. Treat the video camera as 'one of the audience'.
Later, if you video recorded your presentation, watch it first with the sound off. Consider the following:

- the appearance and design of the visual
- your body position in relation to 'the audience'
- any gestures, use of hands, etc.
- your maintaining eye contact.

Now either watch your video recording with the sound on or listen to the audio recording. Consider the following:

- the clarity of your message
- the appropriacy of the words you used
- highlighting of the main facts
- the amount of detail – not too much.

Language Checklist

Using visuals

Types of visual support
visual
film / video
picture / diagram
pie chart
– segment
chart / table
– row / column
graph / bar graph / line graph
– x axis or horizontal axis
– y axis or vertical axis
– left-hand / right-hand axis
lines (in a line graph)
– solid line
– dotted line
– broken line

Comparisons
This compares *x* with *y*
Let's compare the …
Here you see a comparison between …

Equipment
(slide) projector
– slides (Br. Eng.)
– diapositives (Am. Eng.)

computer tools
– laptop
– data projector
– monitor
– PowerPoint
– modem
– Internet download
overhead projector (OHP)
– transparency (Br. Eng.)
– slide (Am. Eng.)
flip chart
whiteboard
metaplan board

Introducing a visual
I'd like to show you …
Have a look at this …
This (graph) shows / represents …
Here we can see …
Let's look at this …
Here you see the trend in …

Describing trends

to go up to increase to rise to climb to improve	 an increase a rise a climb an improvement	to go down to decrease to fall to decline to deteriorate	 a decrease a fall a decline a deterioration
to recover to get better	a recovery an upturn	 to get worse	 a downturn
to level off to stabilise to stay the same	a levelling off		
to reach a peak to reach a maximum to peak	a peak	to reach a low point to hit bottom	
to undulate to fluctuate	an undulation a fluctuation		

Describing the speed of change

a dramatic a marked a significant a slight	increase / fall	to increase / fall	dramatically markedly slightly significantly

Skills Checklist

Using visual supports

Visuals must be:
- well prepared
- well chosen
- clear

Available media

Use media which suit the room and audience size.
- overhead projector (OHP)
  – transparencies / OHTs / slides (Am. Eng.)
- slide projector
  – slides / diapositives (Am. Eng.)
- video / computer graphics / flip chart / whiteboard
- computer / PowerPoint
- Internet

Use of visual aids

Combination of OHP and flip chart with pens often good.
First visual should give the title of talk.
Second should show structure of talk – main headings.
Keep text to minimum – never just read text from visuals.
Do not use too many visuals – guide is one per minute.
Use pauses – give audience time to comprehend picture.
Never show a visual until you want to talk about it.
Remove visual once finished talking about it.
Switch off equipment not in use.

Use of colour

For slides, white writing on blue / green is good. Use different colours if colour improves clarity of message (e.g. pie charts).
Use appropriate colour combinations: yellow and pink are weak colours on white backgrounds.

Use of room and machinery

Check equipment in advance.
Check organisation of room, equipment, seating, microphones, etc.
Use a pointer on the screen (not your hand).
Have a good supply of pens.
Check order of your slides / OHTs, etc.

You in relation to your audience

Decide appropriate level of formality, and dress accordingly.
Keep eye contact at least 80% of the time.
Use available space.
Move around, unless restricted by a podium.
Use gesture.

Quick Communication Check

1 Describing trends

Match the phrase on the right with its opposite on the left.

1 get better
2 reach a peak
3 fall
4 an increase
5 stay the same
6 a slight fall

a) a massive increase
b) fluctuate
c) get worse
d) reach a low point
e) rise
f) a drop

2 Visual tools

Complete the crossword.

1 and 2 Across A talk using visuals from a computer and a data projector (10, 12).
3 and 4 Across The full name for an OHP (8, 9).
5 Across Photographs that you show on a screen using a projector (6).
6 Down A film that you show on a TV monitor (5).
7 Down and 8 Across A board with a lot of large paper sheets fixed to it for writing on (4, 5).
9 Down and 10 Across A board that you can write on with felt pens and wipe off the writing easily (10).
11 Across A 'see-through' acetate foil that you can show using an OHP (12).

3 Describing visuals

Complete the text below, which is from a presentation on changes in the weather and effects on a coastline.

compare see look at
shows clear trend

This picture (a) .... the problem we have had in recent years. On the left you can (b) .... the damage to the coast caused by high waters.
The next two pictures (c) .... the situation now with ten years ago.
Now if we (d) .... rainfall over a 100-year period, it's (e) .... that there has been more rain. The (f) .... is for more rain over the years.

Key
1
1 c), 2 d), 3 e), 4 f), 5 b), 6 a)
2
1 and 2 Across PowerPoint presentation, *3 and 4 Across* overhead projector, *5 Across* slides, *6 Down* video, *7 Down and 8 Across* whiteboard, *9 Down and 10 Across* flipchart, *11 Across* transparency
3
(a) shows, (b) see, (c) compare, (d) look at, (e) clear, (f) trend

8 The middle of the presentation

AIMS

- Holding the audience's attention
- Structure (2) The main body
- Listing information
- Linking ideas
- Sequencing

1 Holding the audience's attention

'First you say what you're going to say. Then you say it. Then you tell them what you've said.'

'All acts of communication have a beginning, a middle and an end.'

1 What are the problems with the presentation above? Suggest ways that you think a good speaker *can* hold the audience's attention.

2 **Read the following passage and identify at least six recommendations about speaking technique which can help to make the message in a presentation clear.**

You're lost if you lose your audience

Clear objectives, clear plan, clear signals: the secrets of presentation success

Any presentation requires a clear strategy or plan to help you reach your objectives. The aim is not to pass away twenty minutes talking non-stop and showing a lot of nice pictures. It is to convey a message that is worth hearing to an audience who want to hear it.
However, how many speakers really hold an audience's attention? What is the secret for those who do? First, find out about the audience and what they need to know. Plan what you're going to say and say it clearly and concisely.

A good speaker uses various signals to help hold the audience's attention and make the information clear. One type of signal is to introduce a list with a phrase like *There are three things we have to consider.* The speaker then says what the three things are and talks about each one at the required level of detail. For example: *There are three types of price that we have to think about: economic price, market price and psychological price. Let's look at each of these in more detail. First, economic price. This is based on production costs and the need to make a profit …* and the speaker goes on to describe this type of price. After that, he goes on to talk about the market price and so on.

Another signalling technique is to give a link between parts of the presentation. Say where one part of the talk finishes and another starts. For example, a well-organised presentation usually contains different parts and progression from one part to the next must be clear, with phrases like *That's all I want to say about the development of the product. Now let's turn to the actual marketing plan.* This technique is very helpful to the audience, including those who are mainly interested in one part only.

Another type of signalling is sequencing of information. This usually follows a logical order, perhaps based on time. So a project may be described in terms of the background, the present situation and the future. Key words in sequencing information are *first, then, next, after that, later, at the end, finally,* etc.

Still another technique which helps to emphasise key points is careful repetition. Examples are *As I've already said, there is no alternative but to increase production by 100 per cent* or *I'd like to emphasise the main benefit of the new design – it achieves twice as much power with half as much fuel.*

A final point concerns timing and quantity of information. Psychologists have suggested that concentration is reduced after about twenty minutes without a break or a change in activity. Furthermore, audiences should not be overburdened with technical details or given too many facts to remember. It is claimed that to ask people to remember more than three things in a five-minute talk is too much. Some say that seven is the maximum number of any length of presentation. Any such calculations are probably not very reliable, but every speaker needs to think about exactly how much information of a particular type a specific audience is likely to absorb and to plan accordingly.

2 Structure (2) The main body

1 Read the following text and identify the following:

a) the relationship between the main body of the presentation and the introduction

b) a recommendation on one way to divide the main body of a talk.

The main body of the presentation contains the details of the subject or themes described in the introduction. All the above techniques are especially useful in making the main body easily understood. They help the audience to follow the information and to remember it. They also help the speaker to keep to the planned structure and to know exactly what stage has been reached at all times during the presentation. Clear structure doesn't just help the audience!

In many presentations the main body can be usefully divided into different parts. The main parts, each with a main heading, are referred to in the Introduction (see Unit 6). Clearly there are many ways to divide the main body of a presentation and often different parts will themselves be divided into smaller sections of information:

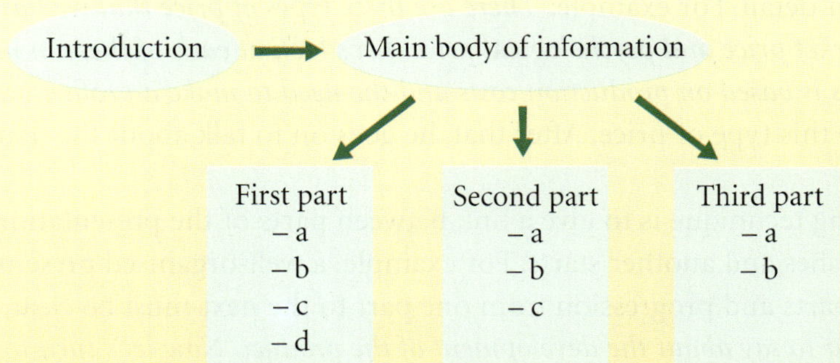

3 Listing information

1 Listen to two presentations of the same information about climatic change. Which is easiest to understand: Example 1 or 2? Why?

2 Now read the transcript of one of the two examples. Underline the words and phrases which list key information and give signals to the audience.

'... climatic changes in the Northern hemisphere may have been the result of three types of effect on the environment: first, volcanic activity, second, industrial pollution, and thirdly, transport. Let's look at these in more detail. First, volcanic eruptions. The 1991 eruption may have contributed to ozone damage causing the unusually high world temperatures in 1992. The second key area is industrial contamination. Industry puts important quantities of noxious gases and chemicals into the atmosphere. There are four important gases released by burning fossil fuels. These are CO_2, SO_2, CO and NO_2. They contribute to the so-called 'greenhouse' effect and global warming. The second main area of industrial pollution of the atmosphere is the release of ozone-damaging chemicals like chlorofluorocarbons and polychlorobiphenols. These are used in refrigeration, some manufacturing processes and in fire extinguishers. Finally, the third source of damage to the environment is transport. Car and plane engines are a problem because they release the so-called 'greenhouse' gases such as CO_2.'

Practice 1

Here are the visuals from a brief presentation to management trainees studying international marketing. Use the information to give a short summary of international marketing strategies using listing techniques.

The Transition from Export Marketing to Global Marketing

Phase One

EXPORT MARKETING

- Home base production and management
- Direct selling to export markets
- Agents and distributors
- Possible sales centres in overseas markets

- *Low investment*

Phase Two

INTERNATIONAL MARKETING

- Production expanded to overseas markets
- Local management
- Cost centres abroad
- Increased local employment

- *High investment*

Phase Three

GLOBAL MARKETING

- Global brand name
- Established in all major world markets
- Global 'identity'
- Cost centres in all major markets
- Complex global production

- *High investment*

Begin as follows.

'Good morning, everyone. I'm going to give a brief summary of the transition from export marketing to global marketing. Basically there are three phases in this transition. These are first export marketing, secondly international marketing and third, global marketing. Let's describe the first phase, which is export marketing …

Now listen to a recording of a model presentation.

4 Linking ideas

1 **Listen to the recording of part of the main body of a presentation on energy resources in Latin America and complete the notes below.**

Topic: Energy resources in Venezuela, Argentina and Peru.

Venezuela → ....

Argentina → .... power and ....

Peru → .... but ....

WHY?

.... and .... factors

and ....

2 **Listen again and this time notice how the speaker links different parts of the presentation. Write in the missing words.**

a) *new topic*

Let's look now at **Argentina**, which is quite a lot different to **Venezuela** in that it hasn't enjoyed such …

old topic

b) *old topic*

That's all I wanted to say about **Argentina**.

Now let's talk about **Peru**. For many …

new topic

c) *old topic*

Now, so much for **Peru**. I now want to say sth about **other opportunities in South America** (*fade*).

new topic

3 **Suggest other language that can be used to make links between different parts of a presentation.**

Practice 2

Choose one of the situations on page 81 to present a short extract from a presentation. Use linking expressions to connect the different parts of the talk.

Situation 1

You are a Project Manager for Stegman nv, a Dutch electronic components manufacturer. You have to give a presentation to colleagues explaining the company's decision to build a factory in Singapore.

Important factors influencing the decision are:

a) local employment conditions:
well-trained workforce, experienced in electronics industry
b) local economic factors and market potential: strong growth in Singapore economy, good location,
business culture, access to South-East Asian market
c) good economic potential in the region, major shipping centre
d) available subsidies, favourable tax environment, government wants inward investment

Situation 2

You are a Design Consultant working for Land Inc., a New York-based financial services company. The company plans to build new offices for its European headquarters in Brussels. There are three tenders for the design. Present an overview of each tender to senior executives of the company.

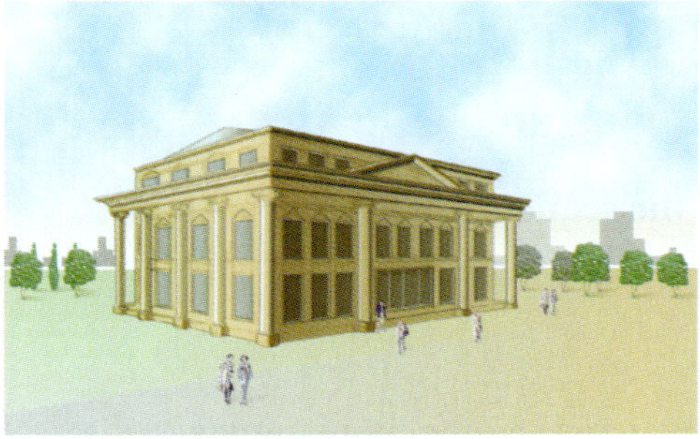

a) **Fox Lee Associates**: British
- $6.0m
- conventional air-conditioning and heating system
- neoclassical design

b) **Shikishima**: Japanese
- $8.5m
- ultra-modern
- solar energy-based heating and air-conditioning

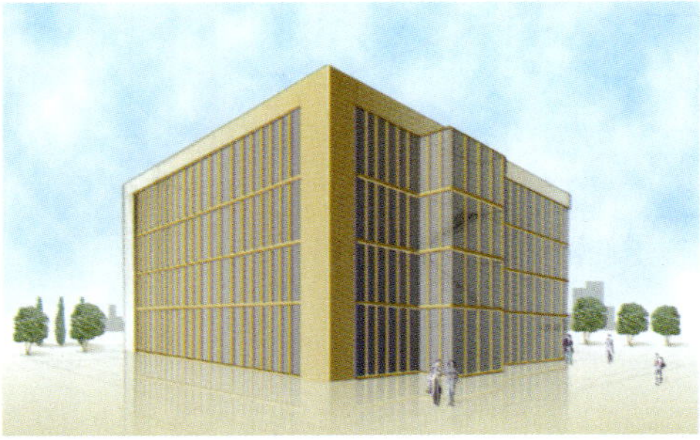

c) **Harald Khaan Group**: Dutch
- $8.0m
- 20% more office space
- low-running costs, conventional heating
- modern design
- exceptional energy conservation

5 Sequencing

1 **Listen to part of a presentation about a construction project in Seoul, South Korea. Number the stages in the project in the right order.**

Put out tenders for construction. ☐
Technical consultation to determine design needs. ☐
Purchasing procedure. [2]
Building. ☐
Put out a call for tenders to architects. ☐
Select the best proposal. ☐
Commission research to find best location for plant. [1]
Period of consultation with architects over details. ☐

2 **Listen again, this time focusing on the language used to indicate the sequence of events. Identify seven words or phrases that are used in this way.**

a) F i r s t o f a l l
b) N _ _ _
c) W _ _ _ _ _ _ _ _ _ _ _ _ _ _ _ _ _
d) The _ _ _ _ _ _ _ _ _ _ _ _ be
e) T _ _ _
f) H _ _ _ _ _ _ _ _ _ _ _
g) The _ _ _ _ _ _ _ _ _ _ _ to

3 **Suggest other words and phrases that indicate the sequence of events.**

Practice 3

Describe any simple process or the diagram below using sequencing language.

Product life cycle

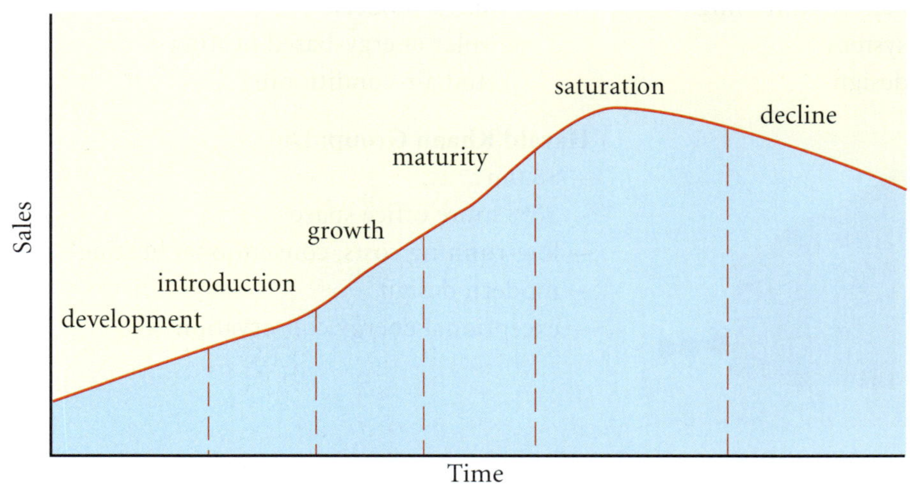

Now listen to a recording of a model description.

Practice 4

Use the information below to give a presentation of about seven minutes. Use listing, linking and sequencing where necessary.

You have been asked by GUBU Inc., a Boston-based toy manufacturer, to advise them on a business plan to reverse falling sales. Make a presentation to GUBU executives. Tell them your recommendations.

Sales of GUBU toys

Introduction

↓

1. Global decline in sales

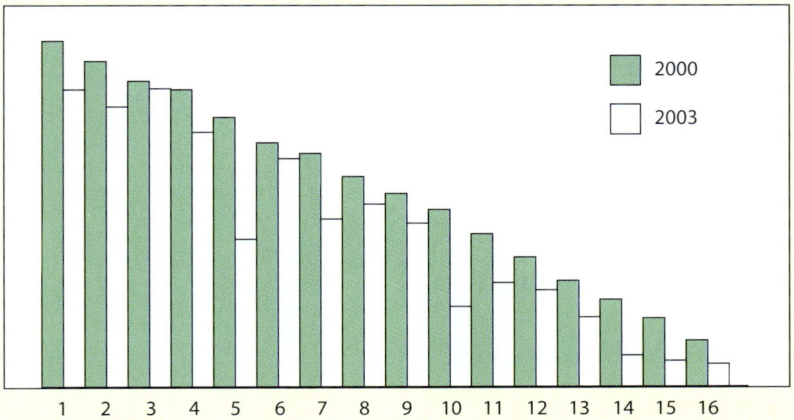

Comparison between combined sales for 2000 and 2003 for 16 products.

↓

2. Reasons for decline in sales
   - poor investment in new products
   - old products losing appeal, not fashionable
   - declining marketing budget

3. Proposed action to reverse trend
   - drop half of existing product range
   - new product investment
   - new marketing strategy with heavy marketing investment

↓

4. Prospects

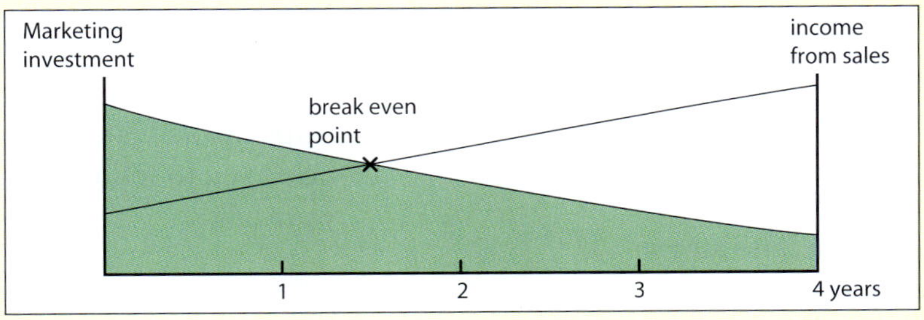

TRANSFER

Prepare an informal presentation on a topic of your own choice.

- It does not have to concern your work or studies but should be a topic which interests you.
- Think about having a clear introduction (see Unit 6) and a clear structure.
- Include visual aids (see Unit 7) if you like.

Give the presentation to your teacher and / or colleagues.

Language Checklist

Structure (2) The main body

Signalling different parts in a presentation:

Ending the introduction
So that concludes the introduction.
That's all for the introduction.

Beginning the main body
Now let's move to the first part of my talk, which is about …
So, first … To begin with …

Listing
There are three things to consider. First … Second … Third …
There are two kinds of … The first is … The second is …
We can see four advantages and two disadvantages. First, advantages.
One is … Another is … A third advantage is … Finally …
On the other hand, the two disadvantages. First … Second …

Linking: Ending parts within the main body
That completes / concludes …
That's all (I want to say for now) on …

Linking: Beginning a new part
Let's move to (the next part which is) …
So now we come to …
Now I want to describe …

Sequencing
There are (seven) different stages to the process
First / then / next / after that / then (*x*) / after *x* there's *y*, last …
There are two steps involved.
The first step is … The second step is …
There are four stages to the project.
At the beginning, later, then, finally …
I'll describe the development of the idea.
First the background, then the present situation, and then the prospects for the future.

Skills Checklist

Structure (2) The main body

Organisation of presentation
- logical progression of ideas and / or parts of presentation
- clear development
- sequential description of processes
- chronological order of events, i.e. background → present → future.

Topic

Main parts	**Sections**	**Subsections**
A	i	a.
		b.
	ii	
B	i	a.
		b.
	ii	
	iii	a.
		b.
		c.
C	i	a.
		b.
	ii	

Internal structure of the main body of a complex presentation

Signalling the structure
- use listing techniques
- link different parts
- use sequencing language.

Signalling the structure …
- makes the organisation of the talk clear
- helps the audience to follow
- helps *you* to follow the development of your talk.

Quick Communication Check

1 Signalling the different parts of the presentation

Match the word or phrase on the left with a word or phrase on the right that has a similar meaning.

1 First …	…………	a) Now we come to …
2 Then …	…………	b) I've finished talking about …
3 Finally …	…………	c) To begin with …
4 That's all on …	…………	d) After that …
5 Now let's turn to …	…………	e) Lastly …

2 Listing and sequencing

Complete the examples of listing below.

There are (a) ………… things to talk about. The (b) ………… is design. The (c) ………… is quality. Then the (d) ………… one is communication.

three / first / last / second

then / one / third / another / several

I think there're (e) ………… problems to address. (f) ………… is competition. (g) ………… is customer needs. (h) ………… the (i) ………… issue is marketing.

Now I'm going to show you (j) ………… examples. Number one from India. Two, from South America and the (k) ………… from North Africa. The (l) ………… example is from Australia and the (m) ………… one is from Russia. Okay, (n) ………… example. India. Here you can see …

first / final / third / fourth / five

3 Linking

Complete the phrases below to link parts of a talk.

1 That c………… the introduction. Let's l………… now at the first part.
2 That's a………… on the theory. Now we c………… to the practice.
3 Now I've e………… the background. L…………'s look next at the present situation.
4 A………… this then, we can t………… to the next part. This is about money.
5 So that's the e………… of the main part of my talk. I'd like to m………… on to the conclusion.
6 I've f………… talking about the home market. N………… I'd like to g………… on to talk about the overseas market.

Key

1
1 c), 2 d), 3 e), 4 b), 5a)

2
(a) three, (b) first, (c) second, (d) last, (e) several, (f) one, (g) another, (h) then, (i) third, (j) five, (k) third, (l) fourth, (m) final, (n) first

3
1 concludes, look, 2 all, come, 3 explained, Let's, 4 After, turn, 5 end, move, 6 finished, Now, go

9 The end is near … this is the end

AIMS

- Structure (3) The end
- Summarising and concluding
- Questions and discussion

1 Structure (3) The end

1 What does the end of a presentation contain?

2 What is the difference, if any, between a *summary* and a *conclusion*?

3 **Comment on the different approaches used by the two speakers in the cartoons. Can you suggest reasons for the different endings?**

4 **In which of the following situations do you think a *discussion* is more appropriate than *questions*?**

- A sales representative's presentation of a new product.
- A chief executive's statement on corporate policy.
- A politician's speech on transport policy.
- A team leader's talk to colleagues on the next phase of a project.
- A manager's proposal to a group of senior executives on improving productivity.

2 Summarising and concluding

1 **Listen to the end of a presentation by Ben Ingleton, Marketing Director of Foss Ltd., an agricultural machinery manufacturer. His talk is about company valuation. What is his key message?**

2 **Listen again. Is this a summary or a conclusion or is it both? Explain your answer.**

3 **Listen again and complete the following phrases.**

a) 'I'd like to end with a short restatement of the main points.'

b) 'So, what are the lessons that we can learn from this?
I think most importantly, we have to build up …'

Practice 1

Look at the following overhead transparencies used in a presentation on safety procedures on an oil platform. Use them to reconstruct the end of the presentation.

Begin as follows:

'That concludes the main part of my talk. Now I'd like to ... '

Summary

1. Three incidents in the year show communication problems.
2. 35% of incidents in the last five years contain some degree of communication problem.
3. Existing communication procedures are not considered satisfactory.

Conclusion

1. Training must place more emphasis on communication procedures.
2. Programme of regular revision of communication procedures should be introduced.

Now compare your version with a recording of a model answer.

3 Questions and discussion

1 **Listen to a recording of two different ways of ending the same sales presentation by Marisa Repp about an automatic warehouse system, the Storo. Decide if they:**
a) invite the audience to ask questions
b) are a lead-in to a discussion
c) invite the audience to ask questions and have a discussion
d) request comments.

2 **Suggest alternative endings for the presentation you have just heard.**

3 **Listen to three examples of possible endings to other sales presentations. Match each one to the comments below.**
a) A **hard-sell** approach, mainly interested in selling the product. ☐
b) **Weak**, as if the speaker lacks confidence. ☐
c) **Customer-friendly**, wants to help the customer. ☐

4 **Read the following text and identify:**
a) a potential problem at the end of a presentation
b) three ways to avoid the problem.

Open for questions: The silent disaster

A nightmare scenario is as follows: the speaker finishes his talk with the words 'Any questions?' This is met by total silence. Not a word. Then an embarrassed shuffling, a cough ... How can this be avoided? A possible answer is that if the presentation has been good and the audience is clearly interested, *someone* will have *something* to say.

Another way to avoid the nightmare of utter silence is to end with an instruction to the audience. This should ensure immediate audience response. Giving an instruction is often useful in sales presentations and where the audience has special requirements. Here are two examples:

A sales presentation
After talking about his or her products or services, the speaker wants the audience to explain their needs and says:

'Okay – I've told you about the ways Snappo can help companies like yours. Now for us to do that, we need to know more about the way you work. For example, tell me about your particular situation, tell me what in particular may interest you ...'

This places a responsibility on the audience to respond – unless of course they have a completely negative view of both the presenter and the message! Assuming they are well disposed towards the potential supplier, it is probably in their interests to offer some information and begin discussion.

A Training Manager

Speaking to an audience of department managers, vice-presidents, or potential trainees, the Training Manager has outlined recommendations and explained what is available. He / She can end with:

'Right! I've told you what we can offer. Now tell me: what are your impressions, what are your priorities and what else do you need to know now?'

Another option is for the speaker to have a question prepared. Ask something which you know the audience will have to answer. This often breaks the ice and starts discussion. It may be possible to single out an individual who is most likely to have a question to ask you or a comment to make, or it may be apparent from earlier contact perhaps during the reception or a coffee break, that a particular individual has something to say or to ask.

5 Handling questions is thought by many speakers to be the most difficult part of a presentation. Why do you think this is? How do you think difficulties can be minimised?

Listen to Penny Yates talking about the difficulties that can arise in dealing with questions after a presentation. As you listen, tick any of the following pieces of advice that she gives.

- Be polite. ☐
- Listen very carefully. ☐
- Ask for repetition or clarification. ☐
- Keep calm. ☐
- Tell the truth (most of the time!). ☐
- Don't say anything you'll regret later. ☐
- Check understanding if necessary by paraphrasing. ☐
- Agree partially before giving own opinion: 'Yes, but ...' ☐

6 A conference on land development in Europe included presentations on financial support for business. Listen to four extracts of different speakers' handling of questions and discussion. Use the table below to mark which extracts are examples of good (✓) or bad (✗) technique. Give reasons for your answers.

Technique (✓/✗)	Why?
1	....
2	....
3	....
4	....

Practice 2

Imagine that you have given a talk on *Marketing in Japan* at a conference on business trends. What would you say in these situations?

1. At the end of your presentation, move to comments / discussion / questions.
2. A member of the audience suggests that you said that many small retail outlets, small shops, had actually closed down in recent years. In fact, you said this process has been going on for a long time. Politely correct the other person.
3. Ask the audience for comments on why this has happened.
4. Agree with someone's suggestions, but suggest other factors. One is the increasing number of takeovers of smaller companies.
5. A member of the audience says the following: 'I ... I understand that a report showed that 700 new soft drinks came out in Japan in 2000 and one year later 90% had failed. That's a pretty amazing figure ... ' Paraphrasing this, ask if in the USA or Europe that could not happen.
6. Someone suggests that in Japan there has always been an emphasis on quality and on products. In the West market research has been more developed. Agree, but say the situation is changing.
7. A speaker says something you don't understand. What do you say?

Practice 3

Divide into groups of four. Each person should prepare, in about two to three minutes, part of a short presentation on any topic he / she knows well.

Describe just one or two aspects of the topic in some detail for about three to four minutes. Then end what you say with a brief summary and / or conclusion. Finally, move to questions / comments or discussion.
Your colleagues should:

- ask questions
- ask for more details
- ask for clarification / repetition
- paraphrase part(s) of what you said
- offer more information based on their knowledge and / or experience.

For each contribution, respond appropriately.

Repeat the exercise until everyone in the group has been in the hot seat.

TRANSFER

Give the end of a presentation on a topic of your choice. Include either a summary or a conclusion and move to questions and / or discussion.

Language Checklist

The end of the presentation

Ending the main body of the presentation

Right, that ends (the third part of) my talk.
That's all I want to say for now on …

Beginning the summary and / or conclusion

I'd like to end by emphasising the main point(s).
I'd like to finish with …
- a summary of the main points.
- some observations based on what I've said.
- some conclusions / recommendations.
- a brief conclusion.

Concluding

There are two conclusions / recommendations.
What we need is …
I think we have to …
I think we have seen that we should …

Inviting questions and / or introducing discussion

That concludes (the formal part of) my talk. (Thanks for listening) … Now I'd like to invite your comments.
Now we have (half an hour) for questions and discussion.
Right. Now, any questions or comments?
So, now I'd be very interested to hear your comments.

Handling questions

Understood but difficult or impossible to answer

That's a difficult question to answer in a few words.
- It could be …
- In my experience …
- I would say …
- I don't think I'm the right person to answer that. Perhaps (Mr Holmes) can help …
- I don't have much experience in that field …

Understood but irrelevant or impossible to answer in the time available

I'm afraid that's outside the scope of my talk / this session. If I were you I'd discuss that with …
I'll have to come to that later, perhaps during the break as we're short of time.

Not understood

Sorry, I'm not sure I've understood. Could you repeat?
Are you asking if … ?
Do you mean … ?
I didn't catch (the last part of) your question.
If I have understood you correctly, you mean … ? Is that right?

Checking that your answer is sufficient

Does that answer your question?
Is that okay?

Skills Checklist

Structure (3) Ending the presentation

A summary
- Restates main point(s).
- Restates what the audience must understand and remember.
- Contains no new information.
- Is short.

A conclusion
- States the logical consequences of what has been said.
- Often contains recommendations.
- May contain new and important information.
- Is short.

Questions
- Inviting questions implies that the audience are less expert than the speaker.
- Beware of the 'nightmare scenario' – total silence! Have one or two prepared questions to ask the audience.
- Keep control of the meeting.

Discussion
- Inviting discussion gives the impression that the audience have useful experience, so is often more 'diplomatic'.
- You still need to control the discussion.

Inviting discussion and questions
- Often the best solution.
- Keep control, limit long contributions, watch the time.

Handling questions
- Listen very carefully.
- Ask for repetition or clarification if necessary.
- Paraphrase the question to check you understand it.
- Give yourself time to think – perhaps by paraphrasing the question.
- Check that the question is relevant. If not, don't answer if you don't want to.
- Refer questioner to another person if you can't answer.
- Suggest you'll answer a question later if you prefer.
- Check that the questioner is happy with your answer: eye contact and a pause is often sufficient.
- Keep control.
- Don't allow one or two people to dominate.
- Be polite.
- Signal when time is running out – 'Time for one last question'.
- At the end, thank the audience.

Quick Communication Check

1 Introducing a summary or a conclusion

Choose the correct word.

1 That *ends / brings / leaves* the main part. Now we *meet / come to / can do* the conclusion.
2 That's really all I *wanted / can / think* to say. I'd like to *recommend / summarise / conclude* the three things I have described.
3 Can I *finish / recommend / suggest* now with some recommendations?
4 To conclude, I'd like to *speak / tell / say* what I think is the most important thing

2 Summarising, concluding and recommending

Change the two paragraphs below with words from the boxes.

Okay, I think that is the (a) ______ of the (b) ______ part of my talk. I'd now (c) ______ to say a few words in (d) ______ . What we have to remember is the importance of good research. In order to get good (e) ______ we must provide enough (f) ______, so I would like to ask for more people and more money. It's as simple as that. Money and people are the vital resources we need. That's all.

main
end
conclusion
like
resources
information

summarise
said
concludes
then
described
conclusion
first

That (g) ______ what I want to say so can I (h) ______ the main points? (i) ______ I talked about the objectives of the Calypso project. (j) ______ I (k) ______ the problems, essentially the lack of resources and the time difficulties we had. We also had personnel problems. Finally I (l) ______ that during this time, our competitors have introduced new products. In (m) ______, therefore, it is now extremely important to launch a new Calypso product during the current year. Thank you for listening.

3 Introducing questions and discussion

Make correct phrases by matching the verb on the left to the correct words on the right.

1 conclude	b	a) your views
2 hear	______	b) my talk
3 have time	______	c) some comments
4 make	______	d) a question
5 ask	______	e) for a discussion

Key
1
1 ends, come to, 2 wanted, summarise, 3 finish, 4 say
2
(a) end, (b) main, (c) like, (d) conclusion, (e) information, (f) resources, (g) concludes, (h) summarise, (i) First, (j) Then, (k) described, (l) said, (m) conclusion
3
1 b), 2 a), 3 e), 4 c), 5 d)

MODULE 4

MEETINGS

10 Making meetings effective

AIMS

- What makes a good meeting?
- Chairing a meeting
- Establishing the purpose of a meeting

1 What makes a good meeting?

Some comments on business meetings:

'Two or more people getting together for a specific business purpose.'
Gower Publishing Ltd., 1988. Extracted from *The Gower Handbook of Management*, p. 1185.

'The fewer the merrier.'
© Milo O. Frank 1989. Extracted from *How to Run a Successful Meeting in Half the Time* published by Corgi, a division of Transworld Publishers Ltd. All rights reserved.

1 **What makes a good meeting? Suggest what you think are the characteristics of a successful meeting.**

2 **Listen to the recording of Allan Case, an engineer, talking about the characteristics of successful business meetings. He makes *five* of the eight points below. Identify the correct order of these points.**

There is a written agenda.	☐
Clear objectives – known to everyone.	☐
Respect for the time available / time-planning.	☐
Good chair – effective control.	☐
Emotions are kept under control.	☐
Good preparation.	☐
Everyone gets to say what they need to say.	☐
Reaching objectives.	☐

2 Chairing a meeting

'Mr. Skelton, can I go out and play now?'

What do you think the functions of the chairperson are during a meeting?

1 **Listen to a recording of a meeting at Hilo Co., a small subsidiary of a multinational company. The meeting is to discuss the decline in profits. Listen once. Say which of the following are given as reasons for the fall.**

Prices are too high.	Yes / No
The company has wasted money on research and development.	Yes / No
Sales are down.	Yes / No
The sales budget is too low.	Yes / No
No one likes the Chief Sales Executive.	Yes / No
The products are old.	Yes / No

2 **Listen again, paying attention to the role of the chair in the discussion. Tick (✓) which of the following functions the chair performs at this meeting.**

Thanks people for coming.	☐	Prevents interruptions.	☐
Starts the meeting on time.	☐	Makes people stick to the subject.	☐
States the objective.	☐	Gives a personal opinion.	☐
Refers to the agenda.	☐	Summarises.	☐
Changes the agenda.	☐	Asks for comments.	☐
Talks about a previous meeting.	☐	Decides when to have a break.	☐
Introduces the first speaker.	☐	Closes the meeting.	☐

3 Suggest phrases which could be used by a chairperson in the following situations in a meeting.

a) To welcome the participants to a meeting.
b) To state the objectives of the meeting.
c) To introduce the agenda.
d) To introduce the first speaker.
e) To prevent an interruption.
f) To thank a speaker for his / her contribution.
g) To introduce another speaker.
h) To keep discussion to the relevant issues.
i) To summarise discussion.
j) To ask if anyone has anything to add.
k) To suggest moving to the next topic on the agenda.
l) To summarise certain actions that must be done following the meeting (for example, do research, write a report, meet again, write a letter, etc.).
m) To close the meeting.

Practice 1

Work in groups of four. Decide on a chair and have a brief meeting using one of the situations below.

After a few minutes' preparation, the chair starts the meeting, introduces the agenda, invites the first speaker to make his / her proposal, prevents interruptions, brings in other speakers, summarises, etc.

Situation 1

Meeting

To identify ways to advertise clothes and lifestyle products to youth markets in Europe

Time: Finish:
Place: Participants:

Agenda

1. Budget to be decided at a later meeting.
2. Preferred markets: Suggestion: Eurozone, especially France, Germany, Italy and Spain.
3. Advertising media: Lifestyle magazines / television / Internet / sports sponsorship / others? *Note: TV advertising is the most expensive.*

Situation 2

Meeting

To decide on training needs and how to spend $100,000 on training.

Time: Finish:
Place: Participants:

Agenda

1. Decide priorities: marketing / information technology / languages.
2. Allocate costs.
3. Decide outline programme.

3 Establishing the purpose of a meeting

1 Below is an incomplete agenda for a meeting of an environmental research unit. Listen to the recording of the start of the meeting. You will hear the opening remarks from the chair, Victor Allen. Note the objectives of the meeting by filling in the spaces in the agenda.

> **Environmental Research Unit**
>
> Quarterly Meeting
>
> 24th May 20—
> Room A 32, South Side Science Park
>
> Participants: Victor Allen (Chair), Sonia Sandman, Vince Camden, Russell James.
> Time: 10.00 Finish: 12.00
>
> **Agenda**
>
> 1. (a) ______________ present projects
>
> 1.1 Hydroclear
> 1.2 PCB reduction
>
> 2. (b) ______________
>
> 3. (c) ______________
>   – Government
>   – United Nations / World Health Organization
>   – Industry

Practice 2

1 **In groups, work out a brief agenda, with an appropriate order, for a meeting of the marketing department of Axis Finance Ltd., a medium-sized financial services company. Your agenda should include the points listed here:**

- any other business
- minutes of previous meeting
- date of next meeting
- personnel changes
- chair's opening address
- new products
- marketing plans for next year
- review of marketing performance in the current year
- apologies for absence.

2 **In pairs, prepare a brief opening statement by the chair to introduce the meeting above:**

- think about what the opening statement from the Chair needs to say
- use your agenda as a guide
- refer to the Language Checklist
- practise in pairs.

Role play

Work in groups of four.

Ash & Whitebeam is a manufacturing company. The Board has decided to set up a subcommittee to examine the four problems contained in File cards 20–23.

Your group is that subcommittee and you are meeting to discuss these problems and to make recommendations to the Board. Read through the information on the File cards. Decide in groups who should lead discussion on each of the four topics. Each group member should prepare his / her introduction. When everyone is ready, begin the meeting. If possible, also choose an overall Chair for the meeting.

TRANSFER 1

Think about the role play meeting that you have worked on in this unit and your role in it. Evaluate the meeting by considering the following:

- What were the objectives?
- What was your role in the meeting?
- Did you use any visual supports?
- What was the result of the meeting?
- How did you feel about this result?
- What action or follow-up was agreed?

TRANSFER 2

If you were the Chair of the meeting, again think about your role. Consider all the above questions but also the following:

- What were the objectives?
- How long did it take – was this too long or too short?
- Were you an effective Chair?
- Did you summarise the meeting?
- How could you have chaired the meeting better?

TRANSFER 3

If you know of any meeting that you are going to participate in, think about your preparation for that meeting. What do you need to consider?

Language Checklist

Chairing and leading discussion

Opening the meeting
Thank you for coming …
(It's five o'clock). Let's start …
We've received apologies from …
Any comments on our previous meeting?

Introducing the agenda
You've all seen the agenda …
On the agenda, you'll see there are three items.
There is one main item to discuss …

Stating objectives
We're here today to hear about plans for …
Our objective is to discuss different ideas …
What we want to do today is to reach a decision …

Introducing discussion
The background to the problem is …
This issue is about …
The point we have to understand is …

Calling on a speaker
I'd like to ask Mary to tell us about …
Can we hear from Mr Passas on this?
I know that you've prepared a statement on your Department's views …

Controlling the meeting
Sorry Hans, can we let Magda finish?
Er, Henry, we can't talk about that now.

Summarising
So, what you're saying is …
Can I summarise that? You mean …
So, the main point is …

Moving the discussion on
Can we go on to think about …
Let's move on to the next point.

Closing the meeting
I think we've covered everything.
So, we've decided …
I think we can close the meeting now.
That's it. The next meeting will be …

Skills Checklist

Preparation for meetings

Chair
- Decide objectives.
- What type of meeting (formal or informal, short or long, regular or a 'one-off', internal / external information-giving / discussion / decision-making)?
- Is a social element required?
- Prepare an agenda.
- Decide time / place / participants / who must attend and who can be notified of decisions.
- Study subjects for discussion.
- Anticipate different opinions.
- Speak to participants.

Secretary
- Obtain agenda and list of participants.
- Inform participants and check:
  - room, equipment, paper, materials.
  - refreshments, meals, accommodation, travel.

Participants
- Study subjects on agenda, work out preliminary options.
- If necessary, find out team or department views.
- Prepare own contribution, ideas, visual supports, etc.

The role of the Chair
- Start and end on time.
- Introduce objectives, agenda.
- Introduce speakers.
- Define time limits for contributions.
- Control discussion, hear all views.
- Summarise discussion at key points.
- Ensure that key decisions are written down by the secretary.
- Ensure that conclusions and decisions are clear and understood.
- Define actions to be taken and individual responsibilities.

Quick Communication Check

1 Meetings vocabulary

Look at the word square below. Find seven words which match the given definitions.

1 A written report of what was said in a meeting.
2 People who attend a meeting.
3 The purpose or intention of the meeting.
4 List of items to discuss in a meeting.
5 Person who controls a meeting.
6 Change the date of a meeting to a later date.
7 To have a break in a meeting.

P	A	R	T	I	C	I	P	A	N	T	S
F	G	I	O	I	H	P	H	O	V	N	O
A	E	M	J	C	A	Y	S	B	D	N	M
N	N	O	A	Z	I	B	E	J	E	O	I
D	D	C	N	P	R	A	S	E	D	N	M
E	A	K	C	O	B	J	E	C	H	I	N
K	A	B	M	S	O	P	C	T	Y	X	Q
D	A	B	C	T	H	H	O	I	L	T	U
R	D	B	N	P	L	K	P	V	O	O	I
I	A	D	J	O	U	R	N	E	D	J	S
G	D	M	I	N	U	T	E	S	Z	M	T
T	U	N	B	E	A	R	T	S	A	P	P

2 Chairing a meeting

A Complete the following sentences with words from the box.

report
finish
agenda
purpose
move on
items
close
summarise
questions
postpone
discussion
welcome

1 .... to the meeting.
2 We have three .... on the ....
3 The main .... of the meeting is to reach a decision on the Abacus Project.
4 I'd like to hear John's .... and then we can have a ....
5 I hope we can .... by 4 o'clock.
6 John, can you .... your main points?
7 Does anyone have any ....?
8 Let's .... to the next point.
9 There is not enough time to discuss this. Can we .... this discussion to another meeting?
10 I think we should .... the meeting now, as it's after 4 o'clock.

B Choose the right ending to make the chair's remarks below.

1 I'd like to welcome .... a) who is going to present a short report.
2 There are three things .... b) comments on Marie's report?
3 Can I introduce Marie Fischer, ... c) all the items on the agenda.
4 Does anyone have any .... d) a date for our next meeting?
5 Let's move .... e) for coming.
6 So, that's completed .... f) to the next point.
7 Can we fix .... g) all for today.
8 I think that's .... h) on the agenda.
9 Thanks .... i) everyone to the meeting.

Key

1

P	A	R	T	I	C	I	P	A	N	T	S
F	G	I	O	I	H	P	H	O	V	N	O
A	E	M	J	C	A	Y	S	B	D	N	M
N	N	O	A	Z	I	B	E	J	E	O	I
D	D	C	N	P	R	A	S	E	D	N	M
E	A	K	C	O	B	J	E	C	H	I	N
K	A	B	M	S	O	P	C	T	Y	X	Q
D	A	B	C	T	H	H	O	I	L	T	U
R	D	B	N	P	L	K	P	V	O	O	I
I	A	D	J	O	U	R	N	E	D	J	S
G	D	M	I	N	U	T	E	S	Z	M	T
T	U	N	B	E	A	R	T	S	A	P	P

2

A

1 Welcome, 2 items, agenda, 3 purpose, 4 report, discussion, 5 finish, 6 summarise, 7 questions, 8 move on, 9 postpone, 10 close

B

1 i), 2 h), 3 a), 4 b), 5 f), 6 c), 7 d), 8 g), 9 e)

11 Sorry to interrupt, but ...

AIMS
- The structure of decision-making
- Stating and asking for opinion
- Interrupting and handling interruptions

1 The structure of decision-making

1 Read the following extract and answer these questions.
a) What kind of meetings is the text about?
b) What *structure* does the text describe?
c) What key point is made about communication?

2 Read the text again. Do you agree with:
a) the first sentence? Give reasons for your answer.
b) Haynes's suggestions for the steps involved in decision-making?
c) the view that communication must be a two-way process?
d) what the writer says about consensus in the final paragraph?

The reason for having a meeting is to make a decision. Information may be given in a presentation followed by questions or discussion, but it is to get a consensus that the meeting has been arranged in the first place. Achieving this in the most time- and cost-effective manner possible is a goal that everyone attending (the meeting) must share.

Marion Haynes (1988) maintains that decision-making meetings need to follow a specific structure. The rational decision process includes the following steps:

- study / discuss / analyse the situation
- define the problem
- set an objective
- state imperatives and desirables
- generate alternatives
- establish evaluation criteria
- evaluate alternatives
- choose among alternatives.

One other aspect of decision-making is the necessity for participants in the meeting to be aware of one another's needs and perceptions. If these are not effectively communicated, if there is an insufficient degree of understanding of one another's requirements, then an acceptable conclusion is unlikely to be reached. There are four essential elements in decision-making: awareness, understanding, empathy and perception.

It is only when we accept that communications are a two-way process that any form of communication, including decision-making, will become genuinely successful and effective.

Decision-making is not always an identifiable activity. Frequently the discussion can evolve into a consensus which can be recognised and verbalised by the leader without the need to 'put things to the vote'.

Adapted from Bernice Hurst *The Handbook of Communication Skills* (London: Kogan Page, 1991).

3 **Find words or phrases in the text which mean the same as the following:**

a) common agreement
b) economical use of resources
c) aim
d) fix a goal
e) what one must have
f) what one would like to have
g) consider other options
h) way of seeing things
i) seeing things as others see them
j) develop
k) express through speaking.

2 Stating and asking for opinion

1 **Quickly suggest as many ways of asking for opinion and stating opinion as you can. Two examples are given here:**

What do you think about … ? – I think …

Do you have any opinion on … ? – In my experience …

2 **Listen to a recording of directors of a pharmaceuticals company discussing buying new production control equipment. They have to choose between two alternative suppliers, A and B. As you listen, refer to the graph below which shows the market share development of suppliers A and B.**

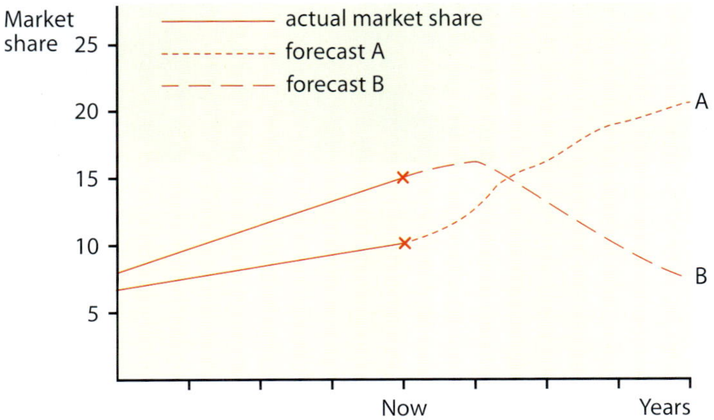

Comparison of projected market share: Companies A and B

a) In technical terms, which system is better?
b) Which is the cheapest?
c) Which system seems to be the best choice? Why?

3 **Listen again. Identify examples of language used to:**
a) ask for opinion
b) state opinion.

Did you think of these in Exercise 1?

Practice 1

Below are a series of topics. Ask colleagues for their views and note if their opinions are weak, strong or neutral. If asked, give your views on the subjects – either quite strongly or fairly weakly.

1 Arms trade

Your opinion ....

Others' opinion ....

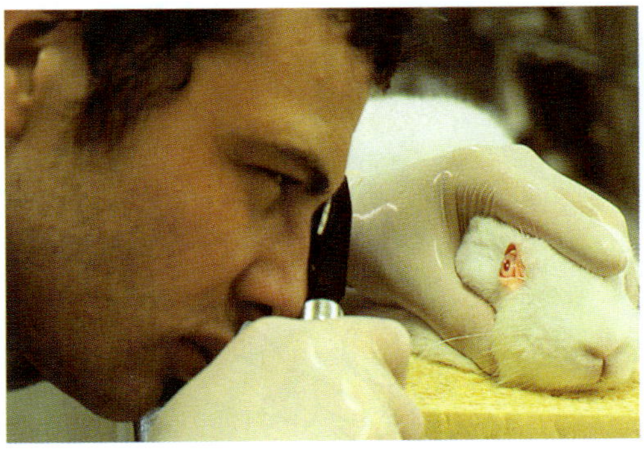

2 Testing cosmetic products on animals

Your opinion ....

Others' opinion ....

3 **Expenditure on space research**

Your opinion ....

Others' opinion ....

4 **Exploitation of the rainforests**

Your opinion ....

Others' opinion ....

5 **The quality of television broadcasting**

Your opinion ....

Others' opinion ....

6 **Nuclear power**

Your opinion ....

Others' opinion ....

3 Interrupting and handling interruptions

1 Listen to the recording of a discussion in the European sales office of an American off-road automobile manufacturer, Amass. It concerns the advertising plans for the launch of a new truck, the Rodeo 4 PLUS. The Marketing Manager, Matt Haslam, is explaining his ideas. Mark the following statements as True (T) or False (F).

a) The truck will be sold to professional users of off-road vehicles. ☐
b) It is not going to be used as a mass market on-road vehicle. ☐
c) Matt wants to keep the same agency they have always used. ☐
d) Matt used his own research to help him make decisions. ☐
e) Changing advertising agency would cost 50% more. ☐

2 Listen again. Number the following interrupting phrases in the order in which you hear them.

a) Yes, but Matt, if I can interrupt you again. We're talking serious money here. We've got to be careful … ☐
b) Er, excuse me, Matt, just a moment. That's a big claim … ☐
c) It's the most important thing … ☐
d) One moment! Can we start with a few basics? ☐
e) Yes, so, a select, professional market first, then the mass market, an on-road vehicle. ☐
f) But why? CMA have been okay in the past. ☐
g) Let's just clarify where … who the audience are, what's the target group? ☐
h) What! Most agencies charge a lot more than CMA. ☐
i) You plan to use our usual agency, CMA? ☐

3 a) Discuss the style of the Amass meeting.
b) How does Matt handle the interruptions? Does his approach change at any point during the extract?
c) Did you think the interruptions are appropriate?

4 Interruptions can have different intentions:

- to ask for clarification
- to add opinion
- to ask for more details
- to change the direction of the discussion
- to disagree.

a) In pairs, suggest examples of each of these.

b) Below is part of a discussion between directors of an oil company talking about a fall in sales. In pairs, suggest appropriate interruptions to complete the dialogue.

A: The fall in sales is mainly due to the recession affecting world markets.

B: ……………………………………………………

A: Well, it's a general fall of around 5% in sales for most product areas. Also, specifically in the oil-processing sector, we have much lower sales, mainly because we sold our UK subsidiary, Anglo Oils.

B: ……………………………………………………

A: Well, no, I'd rather not go into that. We discussed that in previous meetings. I'd prefer to talk about future prospects. The outlook is very good just now …

B: ……………………………………………………

A: I'm very surprised you say that. In fact, sales forecasts are much better now. Anyway, let me tell you …

B: ……………………………………………………

A: New markets? Yes, but can we talk about new markets later? I have some important information on that. But first …

B: ……………………………………………………

A: Take a break? We've only just started!

5 There are different ways of handling interruptions.

a) In pairs, suggest one or two appropriate phrases for the following:

1 promise to come back to a point later
2 politely disagree with an interruption
3 say the interruption is not relevant or that time is short
4 politely accept the interruption and respond to it before continuing
5 reject a suggestion.

b) Listen to a complete model version of the dialogue in Exercise 4 above. In pairs, match each of the five examples of handling an interruption to one of the ways listed above (1–5).

6 Use the skeleton outline below to recreate the entire dialogue with a partner. Choose alternative interruptions and ways of handling interruptions.

'The fall in sales is mainly due to the recession affecting world markets.'

→ Interrupt: ask for clarification.

Polite response. (5% / most product areas / especially oil processing / also due to sale of Anglo, UK subsidiary)

→ Interrupt: ask why Anglo was sold.

Reject interruption: no time / discussed before.

Try to move on to future prospects (good).

→ Interrupt: disagree.

Respond: you disagree. Forecasts are much better.

→ Interrupt: you want to talk about new markets.

Promise to discuss this later. But first …

→ Interrupt: suggest a break.

Reject the idea.

Practice 2

This task is based on a discussion about investment in public transport. Work in pairs, A and B. Student A should look at File card 13A. Student B should read File card 13B.

Role play

This role play consists of an internal company meeting. It is designed to cover the objectives of this unit and also chairing meetings and leading discussion from Unit 10. Work in groups of between four and six.

Introduction – for all participants
You are directors of a food processing company called Adel Passam Ltd. (APL). The company has been linked with a scandal involving a businessman and property developer called Jordi Cass. It has been revealed that six years ago Cass bought land from the local city authority at 20% of its true market value. He sold the land one year later at a 500% profit. Cass was an adviser to APL at the time as a Property Consultant. The press have suggested that directors of APL knew of the scandal, but said nothing because the company and in particular the founder and Managing Director, Mikel Adela, stood to profit from Cass's deal. Also Cass was – and still is – a friend of Mikel Adela's son, Sam Adela, a director of the company. Mikel Adela died a year ago. Another APL director, Marta Lucas, is married to the man who was leader of the ruling Democratic People's Party on the City Council when the land was originally sold to Cass.

Situation
The Board of APL meet to discuss what action they should take. They are worried that the reputation of the company will be damaged and that its excellent relationship with the local community and its employees will suffer.

In your group, each student should choose a role from the list:

Participants
Sam Adela (Chair)
Jay Worthy (Legal Adviser to APL)
Marta Lucas (Director)
Anton Hassim (Director)
Pat Joyce (Director)
Bernie Callam (Accountant)

The Chair of the meeting should look at File card 24. Other participants should look at File cards 25–29.

TRANSFER 1

Summarise your impressions of the Adel Passam meeting you have taken part in. Classify it according to one of the following types:
- decision-making meeting
- information-giving meeting
- discussion meeting.

How effective was the meeting?
How effective was the Chair?
How could the meeting have been better?
In what ways did the work covered in this unit help with the meeting?

TRANSFER 2

If you have taken part in a decision-making meeting recently – or if the Adel Passam meeting was a decision making meeting – can you identify any clear structure to the decision-making process, which was:
- similar to that described by Hurst
- similar to the DESC model in the Skills Checklist
- of a different kind? If so, what?

Language Checklist

Discussion in meetings

Stating opinion
It seems to me …
I tend to think …
In my view …
We think / feel / believe …
There's no alternative to …
It's obvious that …
Clearly / Obviously …

Asking for opinion
I'd like to hear from …
Could we hear from … ?
What's your view?
What do you think about … ?
Do you have any strong views on … ?
Any comments?

Interrupting
Excuse me, may I ask for clarification on this?
If I may interrupt, could you say … ?
Sorry to interrupt, but …
Do you think so? My impression is …
What? That's impossible. We / I think …

Handling interruptions
Yes, go ahead.
Sorry, please let me finish …
If I may finish this point …
Can I come to that later?
That's not really relevant at this stage …
Can we leave that to another discussion?

Skills Checklist

Participating in meetings

Types of meeting
- Decision-making meeting
- Information-giving meeting
- Spontaneous / Emergency meeting
- Routine meeting
- Internal meeting
- Customer / Client / Supplier
  - first meeting
  - established relationship

Structure of decision-making meetings
- study / discuss / analyse the situation
- define the problem
- set an objective
- state imperatives and desirables
- generate alternatives
- establish evaluation criteria
- evaluate alternatives
- choose among alternatives

The DESC stages of a meeting
D Describe situation
E Express feelings
S Suggest solutions
C Conclude with decision

Goal of decision-making meetings
Objective: to get a consensus in a time- and cost-effective manner

Importance of communication
- Two-way process
- Participants must be aware of others' needs
- Full communication and understanding is essential
- Four elements in communication: awareness – understanding – empathy – perception

Reaching a consensus
- Discussion leads to consensus
- Consensus is recognised and verbalised by leader
- Decisions checked and confirmed

Quick Communication Check

1 Stating opinion

Complete the following phrases.

1 It s………… to me that the price is too high.
2 I t………… the price is too high.
3 I b………… the price is too high.
4 In my o…………, the price is too high.
5 In my v…………, the price is too high.

2 Asking for opinion

Complete these exchanges.

– What's your (a) ………… on this?
– It's a (b) ………… idea.

– Do you have any particular (c) ………… on the subject?
– It's (d) …………, but I need more (e) ………… .

– Mark, can we (f) ………… from you on this?
– I (g) ………… with Madeleine, she's absolutely (h) ………… .

– Let's hear what others (i) ………… .
– Well, I think …

think
interesting
great
agree
hear
information
opinion (2)
right

3 Interrupting

Underline the correct word to complete these sentences.

1 Can I *say / tell / talk* something here? I think …
2 Excuse me, Mr Chairman, I want to *interrupt / disagree / not agree* with what Mr Ancram has said. It's not the case that …
3 I'm sorry, may I *add / interrupt / opinion*? It seems to me …
4 That's not *the true / true / sure*!
5 I'm *afraid / pardon / sorry* but I'd like to *go / move to / continue* another point.

4 Handling interruptions

Replace the underlined words in the exchanges below with words or phrases in the box that mean the same.

talk about   not talk about   interrupt
return   anything to do with
finish   go ahead

1 – Can I <u>come in</u> here?
– Sure, <u>say what you want to say</u>.

2 – Jacques, one point …
– Please, let me <u>conclude</u> what I was saying.

3 – But the agreement is for six months!
– Can we <u>come back</u> to that point later?

4 – Can I ask about the insurance?
– That's not really <u>relevant to</u> the topic.

5 – We should <u>discuss</u> the contract.
– Can we <u>leave</u> that today? I think that's for another meeting.

Key

1
1 seems, 2 think, 3 believe, 4 opinion, 5 view

2
(a) opinion, (b) great, (c) opinion, (d) interesting, (e) information, (f) hear, (g) agree, (h) right, (i) think

3
1 say, 2 disagree, 3 interrupt, 4 true, 5 sorry, move to

4
1 interrupt, go ahead, 2 finish, 3 return, 4 anything to do with, 5 talk about, not talk about

12 What do you mean by ... ?

AIMS

- Asking for and giving clarification
- Delaying decisions
- Ending the meeting

1 Asking for and giving clarification

1 Listen to part of a meeting in which Victoria Lenning, a director of an Anglo-American company, is talking to colleagues about a possible site for locating a factory in the Basque Country in northern Spain. She is explaining the historical background to industry in the region. Listen once and identify the following:

a) two historically important industries in the region
b) the status of these industries now.

2 Victoria is twice interrupted by requests for clarification. Listen to the extract again and follow the structure for the first part of the exchange. Then write in the phrases used for the same functions in the second part.

Victoria Lenning	**Other participants**
The main industries were ... (states idea or opinion) →	Er, sorry, can I add something? (request for clarification)
← Yes, of course. In fact ... (clarifies information)	
↓	
So ... is that clear? (checks that everything is now clear) →	Yes, thanks. (confirmation)
← Now, to get back ... →	(a) ....
← (b)	
↓	
(c) .... →	(d) ....

Practice 1

Work in pairs to complete the following mini-dialogues.

Extract 1

A: Brunei has a tropical climate.

B: Excuse me, ... by 'tropical'?

A: ...., it's hot almost all the year, with heavy rainfall in the rainy season. ....?

B: ...., I understand.

Extract 2

A: Every new product needs a USP.

B: .... USP?

A: Unique Selling Proposition.

B: Er, can you .... what that is?

A: USP .... the special characteristics of a product which make it different and desirable – so consumers will want it. Er, ... that .... now?

B: Yes .... Thanks.

Now listen to a recording of these dialogues.

2 Delaying decisions

Listen to another extract from the meeting about a possible site for locating a factory in the Basque Country. The speaker, Victoria Lenning, is giving more details about the infrastructure of the region.

1 Listen once. Choose the correct answer from the alternatives given.

a) Infrastructure for the region is:
   mostly good
   excellent
   not very good

b) The main improvements in infrastructure are in:
   Vitoria in the south
   Bilbao
   San Sebastian

c) Between these cities there is:
   a complex road system
   a fast train link
   an airport

d) The airport in Bilbao has been:
   rebuilt
   closed down
   made bigger

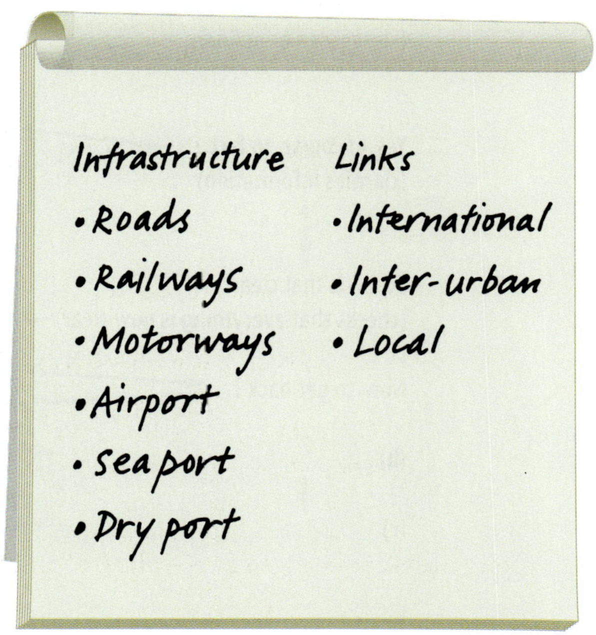

2 Below is part of the tapescript that you have heard. Use your own words to complete the sentences, all of which suggest that a decision needs to be delayed, or more time is needed.

VICTORIA: (a) Well, let's not .... I think it would be a bad idea to assume we're going to choose a city. (b) It .... to think about locating to one of the smaller towns.

FRED: … smaller places, yes. So, should we get details on the possible places?

VICTORIA: (c) We could do that, but we ...., I think, ... a few things. For example, tax benefits, grants and anything like that – for locating to a smaller place, not one of the main cities. Then we could make a better decision.

JOHN: (d) Yes, I agree, but also, ... (*pause*) Er … you've talked about the improved transport links, the trains, the airport, the port in Bilbao. What about the rail links, to these er … the smaller towns? If it's a mountainous or hilly region, it could take an hour – or more – for a truck to get to a main road. (e) So .... at this stage. I think we need to look specifically at the train and road links for smaller towns …

Now listen to the recording again and compare your answers.

Practice 2

You are at an internal meeting to discuss increases in the price of your products. With a partner, use these prompts to make a dialogue. Try to use new language from this unit.

Participant A	Participant B
Ask if the meeting can reach a decision on this. →	
	Respond that we need more information.
← Ask for clarification. →	
	Say we need to know more about the effects of a price increase.
← Suggest doing market research. →	
	Agree. Suggest contacting Hamid (a friend) who knows about market consultancy firms.
← Suggest first looking at previous experience of price rises – then later going to a marketing consultancy.	
↓ Ask for general agreement. Move to next item for discussion.	

Now listen to a recording of a model dialogue.

3 Ending the meeting

1 Read the following text and identify:
a) three recommendations on how a meeting should end
b) what should happen *after* a meeting.

Regardless of the type of meeting (information or decision-making), it is important to close with a restatement of objective, a summary of what was accomplished, and a list of agreed action that needs to be taken.

After the meeting, it is essential to follow up with action. A brief memorandum of conclusions should be written and distributed. Inform appropriate people who did not attend the meeting about essential decisions made.

Finally, each meeting should be viewed as a learning experience. Future meetings should be improved by soliciting evaluations and deciding what action is required to conduct better meetings.

From Marion Haynes, *Effective Meeting Skills* (London: Kogan Page Ltd., 1988).

2 a) You are going to hear a recording of the end of the meeting about a possible decision to locate a factory in the Basque Country. Before listening, briefly discuss what you have already heard from this meeting. Then suggest what the end of the meeting will include.
b) Now listen to the recording. Choose which of the following, A, B or C, is the best summary of the meeting.

A The meeting agreed to locate a new plant in the Basque Country in Spain as infrastructure is very good.
B Concerning possible location of a plant in the Basque Country in Spain, infrastructure is good, but more work is required on financial implications of choosing a city or a small town location.
C Discussion of possible location of a plant in the Basque Country, good infrastructure, no decision yet on where to locate new plant.

3 Think about the recording you have just heard. Do you think this ending follows the rules suggested by Haynes above? Suggest ways that this ending could be improved.

Practice 3

In pairs use the outline below to create a Chair's closing remarks for a meeting. To make this more realistic, add names and other details as required. Practise your closing remarks together.

Indicate that the meeting is almost over.

↓

Check that no one has anything else to say.

↓

Restate the purpose of the meeting.

↓

Introduce a summary of the decisions taken.

↓

Ask if everyone is happy with your summary.

↓

Indicate that (a colleague) will organise a presentation next week.

↓

Fix a date for a new meeting.

↓

Thank people for coming.

Now listen to a recording of model closing remarks.

Practice 4

Work in groups of four. Each group should close one of the situations below. Groups should prepare closing remarks, including a summary based on one of the sets of notes presented here. Be sure to mention any follow-up action that needs to be taken. After five minutes' preparation, form fresh groups so that everyone presents his / her closing remarks to learners who have worked on a different set of notes.

The Chairs of four different meetings made these notes during discussions:

New training courses for telesales staff
Allow £10,000 budget
Peter to identify three possible training companies
Next meeting: 14th March 2 p.m.

Merger of Atlas North with Dransfield
No decision taken
More financial info. needed
Depends on local markets
Detroit subsidiary to present report in 3 months
Meeting in L.A. December

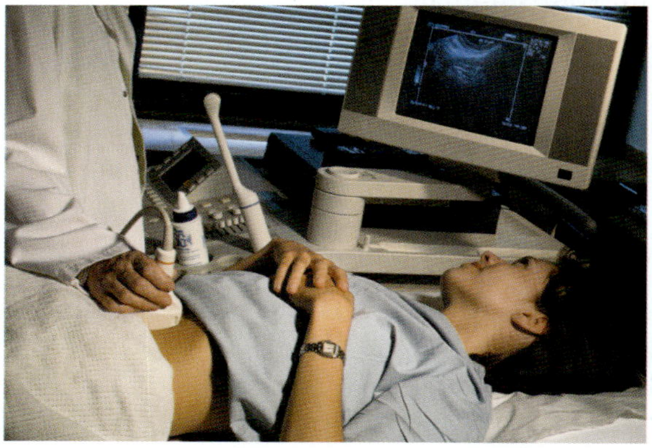

Hospital Management Committee
Purchase of new ultrasound scanner for Intensive Care Unit (ICU)
Commission report on alternatives
Redirect funds from Radiography Unit
Decision by March at the latest
Joan to find out views of affected staff
No meeting fixed

Lawsuit against company for wrongful dismissal of Jane Kee
Accept blame
Offer compensation of $50,000
Personnel Dept. to produce confidential internal report on new guidelines for employees' contracts
Three weeks to complete report

Role play

SOLA
Holidays

Take a family break in any one of our 200 Sola Hotels and have a FREE once-in-a-lifetime balloon trip!!!

Any family booking a Sola Holiday weekend getaway (two nights, meals included) will qualify for a trip in a hot-air balloon – normally worth over $300!!! Sola Holidays will send you an application form for your balloon trip. All you have to do is visit your local travel agents and book a Sola Hotel weekend getaway for any time between now and the end of December, or fill out the coupon below!

Please send me further details on the Sola Holidays Balloon Offer.

Name: ______________________________

Address: ______________________________

Daytime telephone number: ______________________________

Send to:
Sola Holidays Balloon Offer, PO Box 1090, Miami, FL

Don't delay! No need to use a stamp! We'll pay the postage.

This role play is an opportunity to cover work from the entire Meetings module, including this unit. During preparation, look again at the Skills and Language Checklists for all three Meetings units.

Work in groups of three or four. Read the flyer for Sola Holidays above, then decide on your roles from the alternatives given. Study your File card information, the background information below and the agenda which follows. Spend ten minutes preparing for the meeting.

Decide who has which role:

Jan Lubitsch (Managing Director and Chair). See File card 30.
Andrew / Andrea Eastman (Marketing Director) See File card 31.
Fred / Freda Cavani (Director) See File card 32.
Eric / Erica Whitehead (Director) See File card 33.

Background

Sola Holidays is a holiday company specialising in short domestic holidays (not abroad). The company owns a string of luxury hotels.
Sola ran a summer promotion in which any family booking a weekend break in a Sola Hotel automatically qualified for a free balloon trip. (See the promotion leaflet on page 119.) The balloon trips normally cost around £200 and Sola had an arrangement with a balloon company, Blue Balloon, to buy 1,000 trips at £80. Unfortunately, the promotion was incredibly successful and instead of the forecast 1,000 balloon trips, over 4,000 customers applied and qualified for their free trips.

Here is the agenda for the meeting:

SOLA Holidays

Memo: To Marketing
Meeting: Wednesday June 25th 20— 10.00 a.m. – 11.00 a.m.
Place: Sola Holidays Head Office
Participants: JL, AE, FC, EW

AGENDA

1. Report on Promotion for Sola Weekend Getaways
2. Insurance position
3. Action required
4. Any other business

TRANSFER

Evaluate the Sola Holidays meeting and in particular how it ended.
Consider what you have learned from this unit and how it links in with the rest of the module.
Reflect on what you have learned from the entire Meetings module.
Identify areas where you think you have made progress and where you think more improvement is needed.

Language Checklist

Ending the meeting

Asking for clarification
Could you be more specific?
Can you explain that (in more detail)?
What do you mean by … ?

Clarifying
This means …
What I mean is …
What I want to say is …
To explain this in more detail …

Checking that the clarification is sufficient
Is that okay? / Is that clearer now?

Referring to other speakers
As Peter has already told us …
I'm sure Mr Kowski knows about this …
Later we'll hear a report from Neil on …
Professor Gilberto is certainly aware of …

Delaying decisions
I think we need more time to consider this.
I think we should postpone a decision …
Can we leave this until another date?
It would be wrong to make a final decision …

Ending the meeting
- *Summarising*

I think we should end there. Just to summarise …
We've covered everything, so I'd like to go over the decisions we've taken …
So, to conclude … we've agreed …
- *Confirming action*

We'll contact …
John will …
We've got to …
We need to look at …
- *Referring to next contact*

We'll meet again next month …
We look forward to hearing from you …
It's been a pleasure to see you today and I look forward to our next meeting …

Skills Checklist

Ending meetings

Two general rules
Meeting should end on time!
Decision-making meetings should end with decisions!

The Chair should close the meeting with:

↓
a restatement of the objectives
↓
a summary of decisions taken
↓
a summary of the action now required
↓
reference to any individual responsibilities.

After the meeting
- A memorandum should be sent to all participants summarising the decisions taken and the action required.
- The memorandum should be sent to any interested individuals who were unable to attend.
- The Chair should seek feedback on the meetings to try to improve future meetings.

Improving meetings

Motivation to change
↓
Gather information on present situation
↓
Identify specific areas needing improvement
↓
Identify alternative courses of action
↓
Practise new techniques
↓
Improvement model.

Adapted from Marion Haynes, *Effective Meeting Skills* (London: Kogan Page Ltd., 1988).

Quick Communication Check

1 Asking for and giving clarification

Complete the dialogue with words from the box.

understand	exactly	instance
example	specific	want

A What (a) .... do you mean?
B What I (b) .... to say is all the costs are too high.
A Could you give an (c) ....?
B Yes, the advertising for (d) ....
A I'm not sure I (e) ....
B The figures show the costs are too high.
A Can you be more (f) ....?
B Yes, I think we pay about €5,000 too much for magazine advertising every month.

2 Delaying decisions

Suggest answers to the following questions using the prompts.

1 Can we reach a decision today? (No / think / need / more time)
2 Have we finished this discussion? (No / think / need / fix / another meeting)
3 Can you give us the information we need? (No / need / prepare / more details)
4 Have we finished? (No / have / other important issues / talk about)
5 Can we move to the next item for discussion? (Yes / but / not take decision yet; need / more time)

3 Ending a meeting

Finish the following sentences with the correct ending from the right-hand side.

1 I'd like to ....c.... a) happy with what we have talked about?
2 Can we fix .... b) summarising the meeting.
3 Does anyone .... c) summarise what we have agreed.
4 We'll contact .... d) from you again soon.
5 We'll produce a report .... e) has been a good one. Thank you, everyone.
6 We look forward to hearing .... f) another meeting soon?
7 Is everyone .... g) all for today.
8 So I think the meeting .... h) have anything else to say?
9 That's .... i) you again next week.

Key

1
(a) exactly, (b) want, (c) example, (d) instance, (e) understand, (f) specific

2
1 No, I think we need more time.
2 No, I think we need to fix another meeting.
3 No, I think we need to prepare more details.
4 No, we have other important issues to talk about.
5 Yes, but we cannot reach a decision yet. We need more time.

3
1 c), 2 f), 3 h), 4 i), 5 b), 6 d), 7 a), 8 e), 9 g)

MODULE 5

NEGOTIATIONS

13 Know what you want

AIMS

- Types of negotiation
- Preparation for a negotiation
- Making an opening statement

1 Types of negotiation

What do you understand by the term 'negotiation'? In pairs, work out a short definition.

1 Listen to the recording of a conversation between two friends. Identify:

a) the first suggestion
b) the counter-suggestion
c) the agreement.

2 Here is a representation of the typical structure of a negotiation. Compare this with the conversation you have just listened to.

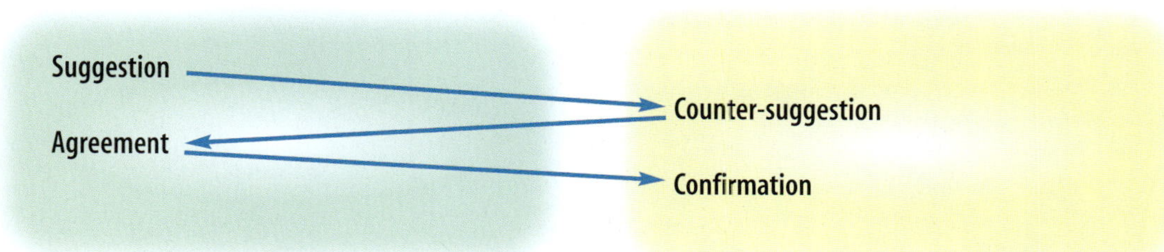

In pairs, suggest a short business conversation with the above structure.

3 a) Listen to a recording of three extracts, each part of a different type of negotiation. Match each one to the correct picture, A, B or C.

b) Listen again. Match each negotiation to one of the three types described below, X, Y or Z.

X – A business negotiation can be similar to a discussion between friends fixing a social engagement. Two parties have a shared objective: to work together in a way which is mutually beneficial. Proposals and counter-proposals are discussed until agreement is reached. Both sides hope for repeat business. This is an **agreement-based negotiation**, sometimes referred to as a **win–win negotiation**.

Y – Two other types of negotiation are less founded on mutual benefit, but on gaining the best deal possible for your side. In the first type, both teams negotiate to **independent advantage**. This means that each team thinks only about its own interests. In this type, a seller typically seeks to sell a product but is less concerned about repeat business.

Z – A third type is the negotiation to resolve conflict, for example in a contractual dispute. Here, it is possible that each party regards the other as an opponent and seeks to win the argument. This is a **win–lose** negotiation.

Discussion

Suggest other situations which match each of the three types of negotiation described here. Think of examples from your own experience.

2 Preparation for a negotiation

What considerations are important in preparing to negotiate? In pairs, suggest as many as you can.

1 Listen to the recording in which a Management Communications Consultant, Diana Ferry, talks about preparing for a negotiation. Mark the seven points below in the order in which she mentions them. The first is already marked as an example.

- Identify your minimum requirements. ☐
- Prepare your opening statement. ☐
- Decide what concessions you could make. ☐
- Know your own strengths and weaknesses. ☐
- Know your role as part of a team. ☐
- Prepare your negotiating position – know your aims and objectives. 1
- Prepare any figures, any calculations and any support materials you may need. ☐

2 Match each of the four aspects of good preparation on the left with *why* they are important on the right. If in doubt, check your answer by listening again to the recording.

a) Knowing your aims and objectives	i) means you can support your argument.
b) Knowing your own strengths and weaknesses	ii) helps clear thinking and purpose.
c) Preparing any figures, calculations and other materials	iii) creates reasonable expectations.
d) Preparing an opening statement	iv) helps you to know the situation or context in which you want to work.

Practice 1

1 Look at the cartoon and think about these questions.

- How could the negotiation have been more successful?
- How would a sales representative need to prepare for a meeting in which he / she planned to ask for a pay rise?
- What would the sales manager need to think about?

'I've come to ask for a pay rise for the team.'

2 Divide into two groups, A and B. Read the notes for A or B below. In groups prepare a negotiation position. Then choose a partner from the other group to negotiate with. Try to reach a better solution than the one in the cartoon above.

Group A
You are sales managers in a large automotive components manufacturer. You are having a meeting with the leader of your team of sales representatives to negotiate new contracts. Sales have not increased in the past year and so you do not want to increase either the reps' pay or their commissions.

Group B
You are the leader of a team of sales representatives. Your pay and commission have not increased for three years. You have a meeting with your sales manager to try to renegotiate your contracts.

When you have finished, report the results of your negotiation.

3 Making an opening statement

Most formal negotiations begin with an opening statement from each side. What do you think an opening statement should include?

1 Listen to a recording of part of a meeting between a small Singaporean software company called LP Associates and a possible partner, Kee Ltd., in a joint venture. You will hear part of an opening statement from Stella Wang, the Production Manager at LP Associates. Tick (✓) four of the eight statements below which best represent what she says.

LP Associates want to reach a final agreement in this negotiation. ☐
These are preliminary talks. ☐
The two parties want to resolve a conflict. ☐
They want to agree on a name for the joint venture. ☐
LP Associates would like to consider joint product development. ☐
They would also consider licence agreements. ☐
LP Associates want to agree a complete sale of their ideas. ☐
They want to consider working on a consultancy basis. ☐

2 Listen again. Complete the following phrases from Stella's opening statement.

a) Well, thank you ....

b) May I begin by .... …

c) First of all, we see it very much as a first meeting, a .... to .... in which we can perhaps …

d) There are two, possibly three, ways in which we ....

e) I'd like to .... these under three headings.

3 Compare Stella Wang's opening statement with the suggestions you made at the beginning of this section.
What did she include that you also suggested?
What other things did she include?

Practice 2

1 Suggest phrases for each of the following at the start of a negotiation.

a) Welcome the other side.
b) Develop small talk (trip, weather).
c) Mention plans for lunch – make your visitors feel welcome (see city centre / local restaurant).
d) Suggest you start talking about the main subject of your meeting.
e) Introduce a colleague (Luke Fox, Marketing Department).
f) Explain general aim or purpose of the meeting (preliminary / exploratory).
g) Say what your side wants from the meeting (establish beginnings of a partnership / learn about supply systems / price variations and supply costs.).

2 Try to bring together many of the phrases above in a single opening statement.

Practice 3

Choose one of the following two situations to prepare an opening statement in a negotiation.

Remember to include welcoming remarks and some general comments on your expectations for a successful meeting and an agreement which leads to a lasting partnership.

Situation 1
Your company, Ultra Compo, is meeting representatives of OHTA Inc. from Tokyo. OHTA Inc. wants to set up an agency in your country to distribute its electronic components.

Objective
Exploratory talks to:
a) know more about the products
b) find out about OHTA's existing international distribution network
c) discuss in general the terms under which the two companies could cooperate.
Independent objective: to internationalise your own company's activities and extend your product range.

Situation 2
You are interested in buying some land in a suburb of Lima in Peru, where you want to establish a distribution warehouse to serve the Andean region of Latin America. You have a meeting with the lawyers acting for the landowner, Puertos Callao S.A., a port authority in Lima.

Objective
Exploratory talks to find out:
a) more about the land, its exact location relative to the port, airport, city centre, etc.
b) the cost of the land
c) the present condition of the land – existing buildings, etc.
Independent objective: to secure the land on the lowest possible terms, either by buying it now for cash, or getting a deal spreading costs over a longer term at low interest, or leasing the land.

Role play

This role play has three parts: to prepare for a negotiation; to prepare an opening statement; to make an opening statement.

You will work in teams. Everyone should contribute to the first two parts and agree on one or two people to actually present the opening statement prepared by the group.

Divide into teams of up to four people, Team(s) A and Team(s) B.

In your preparation, you will need to think about how to establish a good working relationship with the other side from the very start.

Team A should look at File card 14A. You are representatives of Coen Brothers, manufacturers of prefabricated industrial buildings.

Team B should look at File card 14B. You are representatives of Fratelli Taviani, an Italian agricultural feeds manufacturer.

TRANSFER

Either think of any kind of negotiation that you may be involved in at work with colleagues, with your boss, or with another company.

- How do you need to prepare for the negotiation?
- What is your objective in the negotiation?
- Assuming you will not get everything you want, what is your best realistic alternative?
- What is the level at which you could realistically settle?

Or consider a negotiating situation in your private life, for example in negotiating with your bank or with a company trying to sell you a major consumer item, such as a car, a holiday, a house, furniture, etc. Consider the same four questions as above.

Language Checklist

Negotiations (1)

Making an opening statement

Welcoming

Welcome to …

I'm sure we will have a useful and productive meeting …

First meeting

We see this as a preparatory meeting …

We would like to reach agreement on …

One of a series of meetings

Following previous meetings we have agreed on some important issues. Today we have to think about …

We have reached an important stage …

Stating your aims and objectives

I'd like to begin with a few words about our general expectations …

May I outline our principal aims and objectives today …

We want to clarify our positions …

We have a formal agenda …

We don't have a formal agenda, but we hope to reach agreement on …

There are three specific areas we would like to discuss. These are …

We have to decide …

Stating shared aims and objectives

Together we want to develop a good relationship …

We agree that …

It is important for both of us that we agree on …

Handing over

I'd like to finish there and give you the opportunity to reply to this.

I'd like to hand over to my colleague … , who has something to say about …

Skills Checklist

Negotiations (1)

Planning and preparation

Type of negotiation

- towards agreement
  – both teams try to suit joint interests
- independent advantage
  – each team aims to get best deal
- conflict
  – a team aims to win and make the other team lose

Purpose of negotiation

- exploratory (possible areas of interest)
- conciliatory (resolving differences)
- work towards a contract

Targets

- scale (e.g. 1–10)
- decide realistic maximum and minimum acceptable scores

Facts and figures

- prepare statistical data
- know facts
- prepare visuals

Strengths and weaknesses

- list your bargaining strengths
- know your possible weaknesses
- calculate your bargaining position

Possible concessions

- plan your bargaining strategy
- list essential conditions – impossible to concede
- list possible concessions

Opening statements

- state general objectives
- state priorities
- state independent (not joint) objectives
- be brief

Quick Communication Check

1 Negotiations vocabulary

Match the word to the correct definition.

1 agenda	....	a)	a legal document that gives details of an agreement
2 compromise	....	b)	meeting between at least two parties that aims to reach an agreement
3 proposal	....	c)	plan for the meeting or negotiation
4 priorities	....	d)	information used to help make your point in a negotiation or meeting
5 contract	....	e)	agreement that is between the starting positions of both sides in a negotiation
6 evidence	....		
7 negotiation	....	f)	most important needs or demands
8 agreement	....	g)	position (maybe a final one) that both sides accept
		h)	offer

2 Preparing for a negotiation

1 Not all negotiations (or meetings) have a formal a........ .
2 You should know your s........ and w........ .
3 Establish your o........ .
4 Have all the i........ you need.
5 Prepare any v........ supports.
6 Prepare an o........ s........ .

3 About the opening statement

Mark the following statements as True (T) or False (F).

1 Everyone present should make an opening statement. ....
2 The opening statement explains the purpose of the meeting. ....
3 It is a good idea to make positive comments about the other side in the negotiation. ....
4 In most situations it is best to try to work with and not against the other side. ....
5 Both sides usually make an opening statement. ....
6 It helps to try to understand the other side's point of view. ....
7 The opening statement explains your minimum requirement from the negotiation. ....

Key
1
1 c), 2 e), 3 h), 4 f), 5 a), 6 d), 7 b), 8 h)
2
1 agenda, 2 strengths and weaknesses, 3 objectives, 4 information, 5 visual, 6 opening statement
3
1 F. Each side should give an opening statement. 2 F. The opening statement is a greeting and a general statement of objectives. 3 T. 4 T. 5 T. 6 T. 7 F. It is not a good idea to give such important information at the beginning of a negotiation.

14 Getting what you can

AIMS

- Bargaining and making concessions
- Accepting and confirming
- Summarising and looking ahead

1 Bargaining and making concessions

A key principle in negotiating is to give a little and get a little at the same time.

1 Read the following extract. According to the writer, are these statements about negotiating True (T) or False (F)?

a) Decide on the most important and less important issues. ☐
b) Try to guess what the other side thinks. ☐
c) Note answers to the questions you ask. ☐
d) Deal with issues in isolation, one at a time. ☐
e) Make concessions and get a concession in return. ☐
f) Tough bargaining can combine with a spirit of cooperation. ☐
g) If there are problems, you have to accept or reject what is on offer. ☐

Effective negotiating requires clear thinking and a constructive approach

It is necessary to have a clear understanding of what for you are the most important issues and at the same time what for you are less important. Try to identify aspects in the second category where the other side will be very happy to gain concessions. Give what is not so important for you, but is valuable for the other side.

To do this, you have to do the following:

- Check every item of what the other side wants. Ask how important items are and look for flexibility.
- Do not guess their opinions or motives – you could be wrong, or they won't like your speculation.
- Note the other side's answers, but don't immediately say what you think.
- Avoid being forced into considering one issue alone, consider two or three at once – aim for an agreement to a package.

If there are big differences between the two parties, you have a choice of these options: to accept, to reject, or to carry on negotiating. If you decide to carry on, then the options in the next round are:

- to make a new offer
- to seek a new offer from the other party
- to change the shape of the deal (vary the quantity or the quality, or bring in third parties)
- begin bargaining.

Your bargaining should be governed by three principles: be prepared, think about the whole package, and be constructive. In preparing, you must identify the issues, and prepare your bargaining position. You need:

- an essential conditions list – issues where you cannot concede anything
- a concessions list – issues where you can make concessions
- to grade the concessions from the easiest to the most difficult, where you need most in return.

As for the package, you must look for agreement in principle on a broad front. When the time comes for compromise, each party will concede on one issue if they win a concession on another.

The final principle is to be positive and constructive. You should be fair and cooperative, even during difficult bargaining. This approach is most likely to move the negotiation towards a settlement that both sides feel is to their advantage.

Adapted from 'Negotiating', by Bill Scott. *Gower Handbook of Management* (London: Gower Publishing Ltd., 1988).

2 **Read the text again. Identify the following:**
  a) how to respond to what the other side wants
  b) three ways to change a deal
  c) three actions to prepare for bargaining.

3 **Listen to a recording of part of a negotiation between Arco, a German-owned manufacturing company in Ireland, and an Irish research company called Central Auto Systems, CAS.**
  Twelve months ago Arco and CAS agreed a joint development programme to manufacture an engine designed by CAS. However, Arco has recently carried out a major restructuring of its activities. The company has decided not to proceed with the joint venture for the new engine.
  The negotiation is about ending the joint venture and agreeing compensation for CAS. In the extract, you hear Dietmar Töpfer and Erich Rinalder of Arco talking to Celia Spencer of CAS. Listen once and mark the following as True (T) or False (F):
  a) The reversal of rights is linked to the compensation agreement. ☐
  b) Dietmar Töpfer thinks Arco's work on the fuel system must be considered. ☐
  c) It will be difficult for CAS to find a new partner. ☐

4 **Listen again. Identify examples of language used to link agreement on one issue to agreement on a different issue. Complete the spaces in the sentences below:**
  a) We want compensation to ________ our work ________ ________ .
  b) Yes, we ________ ________ to that, ________ ________ ________ we can accept your compensation demands.
  c) So, we need to ________ the question of rights to compensation.
  d) The problem is that ________ ________ revert all rights, we ________ ________ keep the compensation within ________ ________ .

Practice 1

Make sentences which include concessions based on the prompts below. The first is done for you as an example.
  a) a better warranty / quicker payment terms
  We could offer a better warranty if you would agree to quicker payment terms.
  b) free delivery / larger order
  c) free on-site training / small increase in price
  d) 5% discount / payment on delivery
  e) extra £50,000 compensation / agreement not to go to law
  f) promise to improve safety for staff / agreement on new contracts
  g) better working conditions / shorter breaks

Practice 2

Work with a partner. Choose an item that one of you owns and the other would like to buy, for example, a house or car. Work separately to prepare a negotiation based on the sale of the item you choose.
Decide on various bargaining points, including price, extra benefits, guarantees, payment terms, delivery time, part exchange of other item(s), etc.
After brief preparation, begin your negotiation, each making an opening statement before beginning bargaining over the details of the agreement.

Note: You must reach agreement!

2 Accepting and confirming

An essential requirement in negotiating is to be absolutely clear what the other party is proposing and to state clearly what is being agreed. Inevitably, this involves a degree of repetition and paraphrasing. In the recording you are going to hear there are examples of this kind of repetition.

1 **Before listening to another part of the negotiation between Arco and CAS, recap what was being discussed in the first extract.**

In this next extract, Dietmar Töpfer and Erich Rinalder of Arco and Celia Spencer of CAS are discussing compensation to CAS, and a royalty payment to Arco on future production of the engine. Identify:

a) why compensation is important to CAS
b) the final agreement reached.

2 **Listen again. As you listen, write in the missing words.**

a) CAS accepting the principle of a royalty:

We .... a royalty, because once we're paying a royalty we've got an income to support it.

b) Arco insisting on a 10% royalty and agreeing payment of two years' compensation:

Well, ... a 10% royalty,

.... that – the two years' compensation.

c) CAS accepting this:

Okay, in principle .... 10% –

.... compensation based on two years' projected sales.

d) Arco confirming what the parties have agreed:

Yes, okay. So, confirmation, to .... we are agreeing ... we agree a two-year sales forecast compensation.

Practice 3

You and a partner are representatives of Beck Instruments and Ojanpera Inc., a machine tool maker. Ojanpera is in discussion with Beck Instruments to buy a machine, the BI25. Use the flow chart below to negotiate some aspects of an agreement for the sale of the BI25.

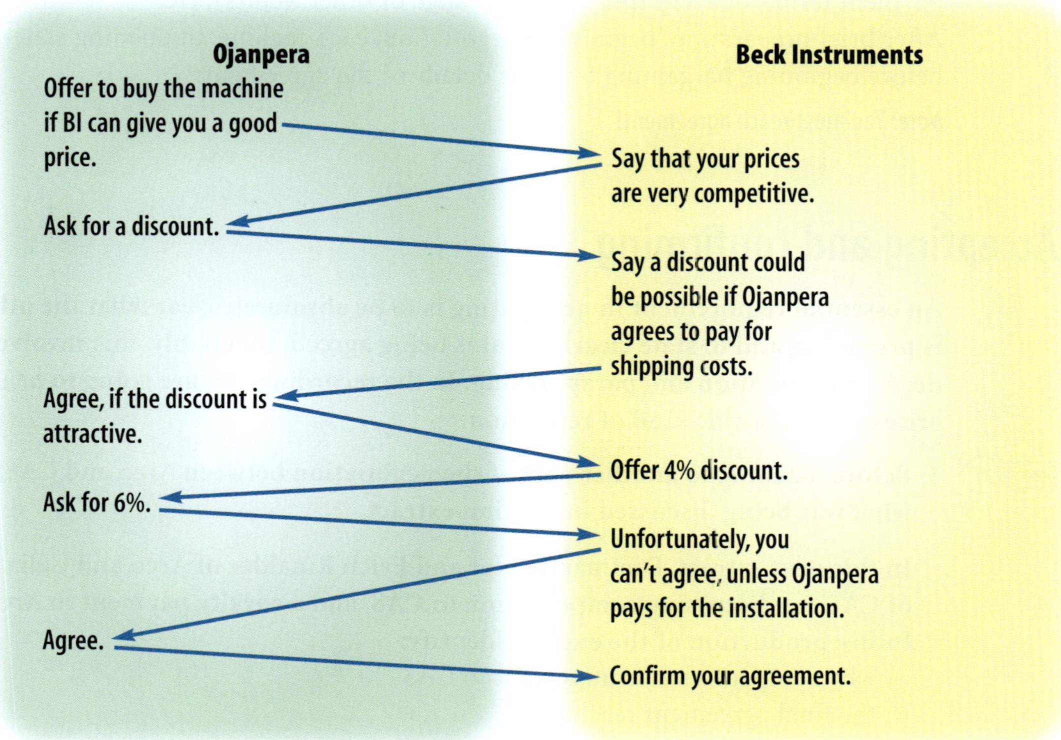

Now listen to a recording of a model dialogue.

3 Summarising and looking ahead

1 **Listen to a recording of discussions towards the end of a negotiation between Jill Kearne from Gibson Trust Ltd., a property developer, and Neil Finch, who is responsible for the sale of a former railway station.**

a) Complete the labelling of the plan of the area involved in the negotiation.

b) What is not included in the sale?

c) What will happen on May 15 and in September?

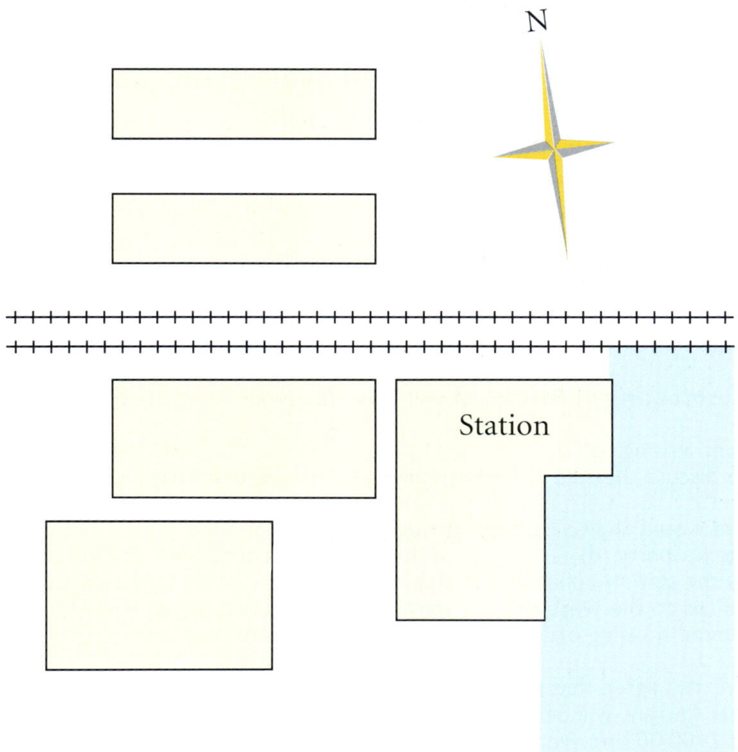

2 **Listen again.**

a) How does Jill Kearne introduce what she wants to say? Complete the following:

Well, ... *– go over the* .... *on. Is that okay?*

… Well, ... *is …*

b) How would you describe the atmosphere in this negotiation?

3 **The following letter is from Gibson Trust Ltd. to a property developer, Aptrans Development Limited, summarising the points agreed in the negotiation between them and outlining the next steps. Complete the spaces in the letter with appropriate words from the box.**

enclosed developed specified examined excluded signed
drawn up confirm included agreed

GIBSON TRUST LIMITED
Units 9–12 East Side Monks Cross Industrial Estate BRISTOL BS14 6TR
Telephone 01272 547777 Fax 01272 547701 www.gibsontl.com

Neil Finch
Aptrans Development Ltd.
140–144 Whitehall
London WC1 4RF

May 2 20—

Dear Neil,

Re: Meeting in Bristol, April 30—'Railway Land Sale'

I am writing to (a) __________ points (b) __________ in the above meeting, held to discuss the sale of former railway land to Gibson Trust Limited.

We would like to confirm through this letter and the (c) __________ drawings that the property (d) __________ in the above sale consists of the land presently occupied by the station buildings and also the former car parks to the east of the station, the offices to the west and the warehouses alongside the tracks. The government-owned housing on the north side of the railway lines is (e) __________ .

We also agree that the station will be renovated by Aptrans Development Ltd. and that Aptrans will be responsible for running an eventual museum and paying a rent of £100,000 per year to Gibson Trust. The remaining land will be (f) __________ by Gibson Trust and later sold off separately. The development is intended to be for commercial and residential use. The eventual use of the land should be (g) __________ in the contract.

Our next meeting will be on May 15 at 10 a.m., at which development plans will be (h) __________ . Soon after this, contracts will be (i) __________ . Then we will need time to consider the contracts but hopefully they will be (j) __________ by the end of September.

Do contact us if you have any comments or alterations you would like to make to this summary. Thank you once again for a very constructive meeting and we look forward to seeing you again on May 15.

Yours sincerely,

J Kearne

Jill Kearne
Chief Negotiator
Encs. (1)

Practice 4

Imagine you are a participant in a subsequent meeting between Gibson Trust Ltd. and Aptrans concerning the sale of the former railway station.
You have made the following notes during your meeting. Use them to summarise and conclude your meeting, looking ahead to future steps.

1. Station Renovation and Use
** approve plans to renovate station as a museum – links to local City Museum*
** museum – operated by Aptrans / all year round*
** gift shop*
** Study Centre – supported by University and City Library*

2. Other land
to be developed by Gibson Trust / agreed commercial 50% and residential 50% – specified in the contract

Next steps: Finish contracts
Next meeting: exchange contracts – June 25 t.b.c.

Now listen to a recording of a model summary.

Role play

Conduct a negotiation, involving bargaining and making concessions and accepting and confirming. Work in pairs, A and B. With your partner, choose one of the following topics:

a) negotiating advertising space at football matches
b) negotiating purchase of a luxury flat in Tokyo's Shinjuku district.

If you choose the first topic, look at File cards 15A and 15B.
If you choose the second topic, look at File cards 16A and 16B.
When you have finished one role play, *either* switch roles and repeat the exercise using the same topic, or change A and B and do the other topic. This way, both parties in the pair can practise buying and selling.
See who gets the best deal.

TRANSFER

Think of a negotiation you were recently involved in. What kind of negotiation was it?
How do you think it went?
Did you keep to the concession rules included in the Skills Checklist on page 140?
If you had the negotiation again, would you do things differently?

Language Checklist

Negotiations (2)

Bargaining
We can agree to that if …
… on condition that …
… so long as …
That's not acceptable unless …
… without …

Making concessions
If you could … we could consider …
So long as … we could agree to …
On condition that we agree on … then we could …
Let's think about the issue of …
We could offer you …
Would you be interested in … ?
Could we tie this agreement to … ?

Accepting
We agree.
That seems acceptable.
That's probably all right.

Confirming
Can we run through what we've agreed?
I'd like to check / confirm / what we've said
I think this is a good moment to repeat what we've agreed so far.

Summarising
I'd like to run through the main points that we've talked about.
So, I'll summarise the important points of our offer.
Can we summarise the proposals in a few words?

Looking ahead
So, the next step is …
We need to meet again soon.
In our next meeting we need to …
So, can we ask you to … ?
Before the next meeting we'll …
We need to draw up a formal contract.

Skills Checklist

Negotiations (2) – Bargaining in negotiations

Concession rules
'A key principle in negotiating is to give a little and get a little at the same time.'
- Ask for concessions.
- *All* concessions are conditional.
- Conditions first: *'If … then … '*
- *'It's a package.'*
- Give what's cheap to you and valuable to them.

During the negotiation

Main speaker
- Create a joint, public and flexible agenda.
- Question needs and preferences.
- Don't talk too much.
- Listen.
- Don't fill silences.
- Build on common ground.
- Explore alternatives: '*What if … ?*'
- Be clear, brief and firm.
- Follow concession rules.

Support speaker
- Wait till the Chair or your main speaker brings you in.
- Be clear, brief and firm.
- Follow the concession rules.
- Support your main speaker:
  - Agree (nod, 'That's right … ')
  - Emphasise ('*This point is very important.*').
  - Add forgotten points ('*And we must remember …* ').
  - But don't make concessions for your main speaker.
  - Listen.
  - Don't fill silences.

Quick Communication Check

1 Bargaining and making concessions

Choose the right alternative from the words in italics.

1 It's okay with us *so long as / whereas* you can supply the goods by January.
2 *If / Unless* the specifications are right we'll be happy.
3 We won't pay that price *if / unless* you increase the quantity.
4 If you ask us to help you then *we'll / we do* send someone immediately.
5 If you pay in dollars we *had to / will have to* pay bank charges.
6 We can offer a discount *but only / however* if you pay at the time of the order.
7 We can reach agreement *unless / on condition that* the price is fixed for two years.

2 Accepting and confirming

A Match the word on the left to the correct meaning on the right.

1 agree with someone	....	a) tie to
2 check (v)	....	b) all right
3 link (v)	....	c) problem
4 issue	....	d) formal written agreement
5 acceptable	....	e) accept what someone says
6 contract	....	f) repetition of something
7 confirmation	....	g) confirm

B Complete the exchanges below with words from the box.

confirm (2)
happy
think
accept
contract
agree
okay
reach

– Is that (a) ....?
– Yes, fine. We (b) ....
– What do you (c) ....?
– We (d) .... that.
– We're (e) .... with that.
– Let's (f) .... what we have agreed.
– Naturally all this will be in the (g) ....
– Can you (h) .... this in writing?
– We're glad we have been able to (i) .... agreement.

Key
1
1 so long as, 2 If, 3 unless, 4 we'll, 5 will have to, 6 but only, 7 on condition that
2
A
1 e), 2 g), 3 a), 4 c), 5 b), 6 d), 7 f)
B
(a) okay, (b) agree, (c) think, (d) accept, (e) happy, (f) confirm, (g) contract, (h) confirm, (i) reach

15 Not getting what you don't want

AIMS

- Types of negotiator
- Dealing with conflict
- Rejecting
- Ending the negotiation

1 Types of negotiator

The delicate art of negotiation

Try to remember the three different types of negotiation described in Unit 13. We may also speak about three types of negotiator: the fighter, the creative negotiator and the one who looks for independent advantage (see the Skills Checklist for this unit).

To find out which one you are, answer the following questions and check your answers with the key at the end.

What type of negotiator are you?

1 Your aim in a negotiation is …
   a) to find the greatest area of agreement in the joint interests of both parties.
   b) to win and to make the other side lose.
   c) to find the best deal for your side.

2 When the other side is talking, you …
   a) use the information you are hearing to identify weaknesses in the other party.
   b) plan what you are going to say next.
   c) listen with maximum attention.

3 You think that …
   a) part of the available time must be spent socialising and getting to know the other side.
   b) goodwill is important but the speed of the meeting should be quick and businesslike.
   c) the meeting should get down to business as soon as possible and reach quick decisions.

4 When you speak in a negotiation you …
   a) make bold and forceful statements, possibly banging the table.
   b) make carefully-considered statements in a calm, controlled voice.
   c) are occasionally forceful and inflexible.

5 If the other side disagree with you, you …
   a) try hard to find a creative position by modifying your position.
   b) repeat your demands and will not concede – your objective is to make the other side give in.
   c) reshape your offer without *fundamental* changes.

6 If the other side state an opinion you disagree with, you …
   a) tentatively suggest an alternative.
   b) ask for clarification and explanation.
   c) ridicule it with sarcasm.

To see which kind of negotiator you are, calculate your total based on the following system.

1 a)3 b)2 c)2 **2** a)1 b)2 c)3 **3** a)3 b)2 c)1
4 a)1 b)3 c)2 **5** a)3 b)1 c)2 **6** a)3 b)2 c)1

If you score 15 or more you are a **creative negotiator**. 11–14 you **negotiate to independent advantage**. 7–10 you are **a fighter**! Less than 7 you should get a gun licence!

2 Dealing with conflict

What causes conflict in a negotiation?

1 **Read the text below. How many ways are suggested to reduce conflict in a negotiation?**

2 **Match each of the following to a phrase in the text with a similar meaning:**
a) highlight the disadvantages of failing to reach a deal
b) think of new benefits for both sides
c) alter parts of what is on offer
d) take a break to consider positions
e) have the negotiation in a different place
f) change the individuals involved
g) ask an independent person to come and help you reach agreement
h) have an informal meeting to talk things over.

Conflict may sometimes be an unavoidable step on the road towards agreement. However, in some cases conflict leads to the breakdown of negotiations as one or both sides realise that agreement is not possible. In many cases this is better than agreeing to something which would be against the interests of the people concerned.

When conflict arises, there are several possible actions which may help to resolve conflict in a negotiation:

- leave the problem, go on to a different topic and return later to the point at issue
- summarise progress and areas of agreement
- emphasise the benefits available to both sides
- emphasise the loss to both sides of not reaching agreement
- restate the issue and wait for a response
- change the package
- invent new options for mutual gain
- offer *conditional* concessions
- adjourn to think and reflect
- fix an off-the-record meeting
- change location
- change negotiator (personal chemistry?)
- bring in a third party (mediator?)
- consider walking away.

Adapted from *The Pocket Negotiator* published by Gottschalk Hartley-Brewer (1989).

3 Listen to a recording of five different statements. All of these are ways of dealing with conflict. Match each statement with one of the following strategies.

a) Adjourn to think and reflect. ☐
b) Summarise progress and areas of agreement. ☐
c) Leave the problem, discuss something else, come back later to the problem. ☐
d) Emphasise the loss to both sides of not reaching agreement. ☐
e) Offer a conditional concession. ☐

4 In pairs, use the given prompts to suggest a response to the statements.

Situation 1
The problem is that we have never offered the kind of warranty you are looking for.
Suggest leaving the point and returning to it later after discussing other issues, i.e. training for technical staff.

Situation 2
There's a number of issues on the table. We seem to be a long way from an agreement.
Suggest changing the package on offer (variables include price, shipment costs, payment terms).

Situation 3
The price you are asking is rather high, quite a lot higher than we were expecting.
Send a signal that you could offer better payment terms.

Situation 4
There are several problems. We think there is quite a lot of negotiation ahead before we can agree on a common strategy.
Suggest advantages of reaching agreement: more global influence, better prospects for the future.

Now listen to a recording of model answers.

Practice 1

A year ago an advertising consultancy, SAR Services, agreed to design and run a twelve-week magazine advertising campaign for KPack Ltd. using specialist journals.

KPack are not happy with the campaign. The first advertisements were a month late, missing two important trade fairs. The advertisements did not appear in two key industry journals. Now KPack are refusing to pay the whole fee for the campaign.

Construct part of the dialogue using the flow chart below.

SAR Services	KPack Ltd.
Offer to run the campaign for four extra weeks.	Summarise the problem – check your summary with SAR.
Say delay not entirely your fault – KPack changed specifications.	SAR were late with proposals. KPack only asked for small changes.
Repeat above offer.	You think the campaign missed two key trade fairs.
	You want a free campaign for next year or you pay only half the fee.
Suggest 20% reduction plus four weeks' extension to the campaign.	Repeat your concerns, explain that missing the trade fairs cost you business.
Partly accept that, but both sides are responsible.	Respond – suggest new solution: 40% cut in fee or free repeat campaign.
Explain your position – Full free campaign impossible.	Suggest an adjournment.
Respond.	

Now listen to a recording of a model dialogue.

3 Rejecting

1 Group Image, a commercial photographic company, is planning to buy new processing equipment. For two days they have been negotiating with Photolab Ltd., a supplier of photographic processing equipment. Photolab have made an offer.

Listen to a recording of a final summing up from Peter Cawood of Photolab Ltd. and three alternative responses from Group Image.

- Comment on each response.
- Decide which is the most appropriate.
- Give reasons for your decision.

2 Complete the following phrases with suitable words. If in doubt, listen again to the last two responses in Exercise 1 above.

a) Thank you for the efforts you have made, but …… very …… .

b) We do not …… at this stage to …… your offer.

c) Obviously, we have …… it very carefully.

d) We are not entirely …… that the technical advantages …… the high cost.

e) We hope you'll …… us again with future offers.

f) I think we are …… to give you a formal …… today, but we will …… to you and tell you of our …… in a day or two. Then we'll …… what the next step should be. So, thank you very much.

3 Match a phrase on the left with a phrase on the right which could be used in a similar situation.

a) Not just now.	I'm afraid not.
b) Not really.	Not at the moment.
c) I shouldn't think so.	I'm afraid we just couldn't do that.
d) I'm sorry but that's not realistic.	I doubt it.

Practice 2

Below are four offers or requests. Reject each one, using the information in the prompts.

Situation 1

Let me make a suggestion. If you agree to buy 100 units every month for the next twelve months, we'll agree a 10% discount.

You don't know how many units you will need in six and twelve months. It might be more or less.

Situation 2

The price we are offering excludes installation costs but does include a twelve-months guarantee.

Other suppliers offer free installation and a two-year parts and labour warranty.

Situation 3

I think the absolute minimum investment in advertising must be $40,000, otherwise we cannot reach enough of our market. It's not much to ask for.

You cannot spend more than your budget.

Situation 4

Now, some excellent news: we'd like to increase our order. Right now you are sending us 350 boxes a month. We need at least 500, demand is very high …

Your order books are full, the plant is working at capacity.

Now listen to a recording of model answers.

Practice 3

Abacus Ltd. is an automobile parts distributor. They want to buy exhaust pipes from Kroll Auto GmbH, a German manufacturer. Construct a dialogue based on the following flow chart.

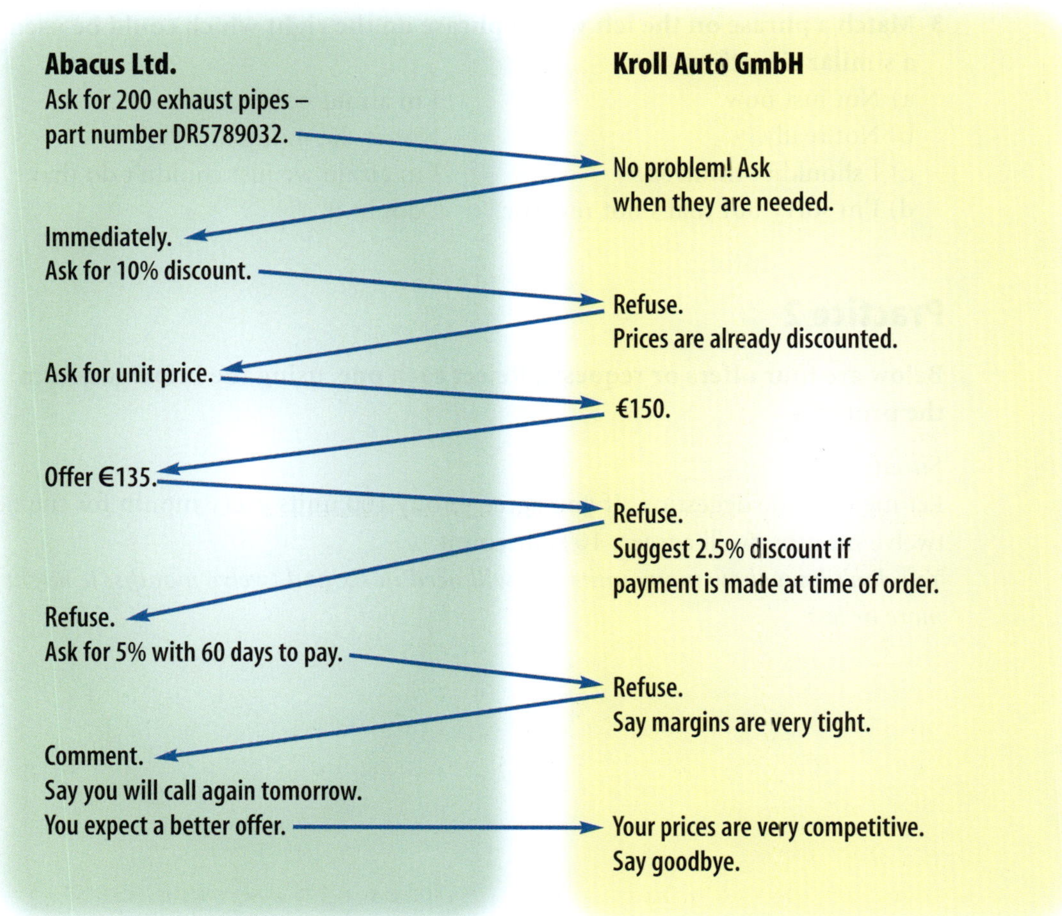

Now listen to a recording of a model dialogue.

4 Ending the negotiation

1 **The words below offer a clear indication of the result of a negotiation. Work with a partner and decide which of these words would indicate a positive outcome and which a negative outcome.**

unfortunately	another time	no agreement	
not ready	fruitful partnership	problems	
very good	satisfactory	sorry	useful

Now listen to the recording to check your answers.

2 **Listen again to the five extracts from the end of negotiations. Complete the grid below.**

Extract	Agreement reached?	Next step?
1		
2		
3		
4		
5		

Practice 4

Suggest what you could say in the following situations.

Situation 1
After a long negotiation, you have reached agreement and now plan a meal in a local restaurant with the other party in the negotiation.

Situation 2
Your efforts to reach agreement have been unsuccessful. It is late. End the negotiation but offer some hope that in the future you might manage some cooperation with the other side.

Situation 3
A colleague has asked you to cooperate on a project, but after long discussion you feel you cannot participate because of fundamental disagreement. It is important that you continue to work together in other areas.

Situation 4

You want to repeat an order with a supplier but they are trying to increase prices by 20%. You cannot agree to this. End your discussions.

Situation 5

A customer is asking you to supply goods in a month. This is physically impossible. End the discussion.

Now listen to a recording of model answers.

Role play

Work in pairs, A and B. A should turn to File card 18A, B should turn to 18B. Each File card contains four different negotiating situations. Negotiate each of them. Let each negotiation follow its course and see if they are successful or not. Use some of the language you have heard for ending negotiations.

TRANSFER 1

Think of examples of conflict in negotiations that you have been involved in.

- What kind of negotiation was it?
- Who was involved?
- What caused the conflict?
- How was the conflict resolved?
- Were you happy with this solution?
- Do you think the conflict should have been resolved in another way?

TRANSFER 2

Think of another negotiation you have been involved in. Was the negotiation a success or a failure? Why?

How would you assess the negotiation in terms of:

- your objectives, targets and limits
- your planning
- the strategy
- team roles and individuals
- the issues
- strengths and weaknesses.

Language Checklist

Negotiations (3)

Dealing with conflict
I think we should look at the points we agree on …
We should focus on the positive aspects …
We should look at the benefits for both sides …
It is in our joint interests to resolve the issue …
What do you think is a fair way to resolve this problem?
We hope you can see our point of view …
Let us explain our position …
Could you tell us why you feel like that?
I think we should look at the whole package, not so much at individual areas of difficulty.
Perhaps we could adjourn for a little while.
I think we need to consider some fresh ideas …

Rejecting
I'm afraid we can't …
Before agreeing to that we would need …
Unfortunately …
I don't think it would be sensible for us to …
I think if you consider our position, you'll see that …

Ending negotiations
So, can we summarise the progress we've made?
Can we go through the points we've agreed?
Perhaps if I can check the main points …
So the next step is …
What we need to do now is …
It's been a very useful and productive meeting.
We look forward to a successful partnership.

Breaking off negotiations
I think we've gone as far as we can.
I'm sorry, but I don't think we're going to agree a deal.
It's a pity we couldn't reach agreement this time.
Unfortunately we appear unable to settle our differences.
It would be better if we looked for some independent arbitrator.

Skills Checklist

Negotiations (3)

Dealing with conflict
- Show understanding of the other side's position.
- Highlight advantages of agreement.

Don't ...
- be sarcastic
- attack
- criticise
- threaten
- blame.

Do ...
- ask questions
- listen
- summarise
- build on common ground
- explain your feelings.

Types of negotiator

Hard
negotiates to win
makes demands

Fighter
↓
win – lose

Principled
looks for common benefits
makes offers

Independent advantage
↓
win – win

Soft
looks for agreement
accepts what's on offer

Creative negotiator
↓
looks for agreement

Rejecting
- Ask for an adjournment.
- Discuss options.
- Remember your limits.
- Decide if your interests are being met: if not, reject the proposal on offer, or suggest alternatives.

After the negotiation
- Compare the result with your objectives, targets and limits.
- Examine the process of the negotiation:
  the planning – the strategy – team roles – the issues.
- Learn from failure:
  – what went wrong and why?
  – identify weaknesses and errors
  – discuss and plan ahead.
- Build on success:
  – recognise success
  – praise people
  – develop teamwork and partnership.

Quick Communication Check

1 Dealing with conflict

Match the word on the left to the correct meaning on the right.

1 compromise .... a) pay special attention to something
2 consider .... b) think carefully about something
3 focus on .... c) agree on less than you really want / a middle position
4 resolve / solve (a problem) .... d) explain
5 have a break in a meeting .... e) find a solution to a difficulty
6 delay a meeting to a future date .... f) adjourn
7 say what you mean .... g) postpone

2 Rejecting proposals

Which of the following words indicate rejection is coming? Mark them with an R (rejection). Mark the others with an A (agreement).

1 Unfortunately … ....
2 Sadly … ....
3 We regret that … ....
4 I'm pleased to say … ....
5 Fortunately … ....
6 I'm afraid … ....
7 It's a pity, but … ....
8 We don't think … ....
9 We cannot possibly … ....
10 I'm sorry, but … ....
11 It's possible that … ....
12 Happily … ....

3 Ending the negotiation – without agreement

Choose words from the box to complete the following sentences.

1 .... on this occasion we cannot .... agreement.
2 I'm sorry we cannot .... accept this ....
3 We .... that an agreement is not possible today.
4 Perhaps if we .... a decision we can agree in the near future.
5 It's been an interesting meeting .... we have not been able to ....
6 We have tried to find a .... but it seems without ....

proposal
reach
unfortunately
possibly
agree
postpone
success
but
regret
compromise

Key
1
1 c), 2 b), 3 a), 4 e), 5 f), 6 g), 7 d)
2
1 R, 2 R, 3 R, 4 A, 5 A, 6 R, 7 R, 8 R, 9 R, 10 R, 11 A, 12 A
3
1 Unfortunately, reach, 2 possibly, proposal, 3 regret , 4 postpone, 5 but, agree,
6 compromise, success

File cards 1A to 19A

FILE CARD 4A

You are a visitor to your partner's hometown. He / She has invited you to a restaurant. *Either* use a menu from a local restaurant, written in your own language, or use the menu below. Talk about it, choose what you would like to eat, talk about the restaurant. Ask questions about the town and what there is to see and do here.

If you like, develop small talk about business, work or the state of the country's economy and / or business prospects.

When you have finished, reverse roles. Talk about your birthplace or hometown.

Finally, when the bill arrives, offer to pay. Final comments on the meal. Decide what to do next.

MENU

Starter

Chilled Andaluz Gaspacho £4.50
A superb treat from Southern Spain. A cold soup rich in tomatoes, cucumber, parsley and garlic.

Roasted Piedmont Peppers £4.50
From Northern Italy. Two halves of red pepper filled with sun dried tomatoes and anchovies. Finished with basil and garlic.

Fish Soup £5.00
A rich broth of fish stock with whole prawns, squid and mussels.

Deep Fried Squid £5.00
Squid rings fried in a herb batter and served with a light salad.

Field Mushrooms with Garlic £5.50
An Italian speciality. A steaming hot dish of quality *porcini* in oil and garlic.

Salmon and Dill £5.50
A Norwegian treat. Smoked salmon from the northern fjords. Served with dill and a chunk of lemon.

Cream of Vegetable Soup £4.50
Fresh vegetables in a rich broth topped with cream.

Tomato Salad with Garlic and Herbs £4.00
Succulent tomatoes dressed in extra virgin olive oil with chives and basil.

Mixed Basque Salad £5.00
From the Basque region of Spain. Asparagus, lettuce, tomatoes, onion and queen olives topped with chunks of tuna fish and egg.

Main Course

Fish

Sea Bream Plaki £18.00
A Greek speciality. A meaty white fish cooked in tomato and onion sauce with lemon and coriander. Served on a bed of rice.

Rainbow Trout with Herbs £16.00
Fresh trout baked in the oven with rosemary and thyme. Served with new potatoes or rice.

Hake with Cockles £16.00
Fresh hake steak fried in oil with cockles and parsley giving the typical salsa verde of the Basque region of Spain.

Thai Fish Cakes with Curry Sauce £16.00
A hot and spicy treat from Thailand. White fish cooked with lime, ginger and lemon grass and served with a spicy sauce.

Grilled Seafood £18.00
A mixture of grilled prawns, cockles, mussels, shrimps and squid, served with garlic bread and salad.

Meat

Sirloin Steak £16.00
Grilled sirloin cooked to your specifications and garnished with butter and parsley. Served with new potatoes.

Fillet Steak £18.00
Grilled fillet steak cooked to your specifications and garnished with butter and parsley. Served with new potatoes.

Roast Lamb £16.00
Oven baked shoulder or leg of lamb with garlic and rosemary. Served with new potatoes.

Spiced Lamb and Cashew Kebabs £15.00
Barbecued chunks of lamb with onions, peppers and cashew nuts. Served with rice.

Rabbit Hot Pot £15.00
A superb stew of rabbit cooked in a rich broth of onions, stout and prunes. Served with baked potatoes.

Chicken with Sherry Vinegar and Tarragon Sauce £15.00
A classic French recipe, fried and served in a deep earthenware dish, with new potatoes.

Chicken Stir Fry £17.00
Chicken breast lightly fried in a rich assortment of chopped vegetables.

Vegetarian

Rigatoni with Asparagus *au Gratin* £15.00
Fresh pasta with asparagus and a cheese topping.

Roasted Vegetables with Couscous £15.00
A colourful assortment of fresh vegetables served with feta cheese on a bed of couscous.

Spaghetti with Oil, Chilli Peppers and Parmesan £13.00
A classic pasta dish from Italy, with a garlic-enhanced olive oil sauce, spiced with dried chillis. Served with fresh Parmesan cheese.

Lasagne Bake £15.00
The classic vegetarian lasagne with layers of fresh pasta in a white sauce with mixed vegetables, mozzarella and Parmesan cheese.

Dessert

All desserts £4.50

Strawberry meringue with ice cream
Apple and apricot tart
Summer fruits cheesecake
Chocolate cake with cream
Caramel flan
Fruit of the day
Fresh fruit salad
Ice creams

FILE CARD 1A

You work for D.F.M., a London-based pharmaceuticals company. You are expecting an overseas visitor with an appointment to see your colleague, Rowena Stanton. Ms Stanton has just used her carphone to tell you that there has been an accident on the motorway – she will be delayed for perhaps an hour.

Explain the problem. Say that another colleague, Karen Pochard, can show the visitor around your laboratories – if he / she would like.

Make small talk – Karen Pochard has not yet arrived either (but you do not have to tell your visitor this). She should be along in a few minutes.

Offer to help your visitor in various ways.

FILE CARD 2A

You work for Caldos, a multinational company. You have arranged to visit a potential partner in a German company. You have received an outline programme for the day, finishing at 5 p.m.

When you arrive, introduce yourself and say you have an appointment.

Also:

- You would like to make a telephone call.
- Unfortunately – you only discovered this yesterday – you need to leave at 4 p.m. as you have a plane to catch (to Paris) at 5.30. You would like to have a taxi to take you to the airport.
- You have heard there are train strikes. Ask if this will affect reaching the airport.

FILE CARD 6A

Someone calls you about a visit to your company. You would like to meet the caller but cannot make any arrangements today – offer to call back tomorrow. Find out who the caller is and how you can reach him / her.

FILE CARD 14A

Team A: Coen Brothers. You are representatives of Coen Brothers, manufacturers of prefabricated industrial buildings. You are planning to launch a major sales drive in Italy, a new market for your company.

The market. The Italian market for prefabricated industrial buildings is very competitive, and since you are based in London and the Netherlands you have transport costs to add to your manufacturing costs. However, you know that on average your prices are 10% lower than Italian competitors, though at the top of your product range, your prices are a little higher than the average, but the quality is also better.

The product. Your buildings are highly functional, and can be adapted to a range of industrial needs. They are built according to strict Scandinavian design quality and use the best available materials.

You supply all materials.

You also take care of the actual construction, including connections for electricity, water systems, insulation and heating.

You can also supply the buildings at finished quality, in other words, fully decorated according to the customer's wishes.

Different qualities are available: basic, standard and ultra, which includes a full range of services at residential quality.

FILE CARD 5A

Select one of the business cards from those presented below. You are the person on the business card. You have been invited to a conference in San Diego, California. You need to speak to Andrea Koss, who is arranging the conference. You want to talk about the programme.

FILE CARD 7A

Select one of the two identities below and call Hamwell Inc. You want to speak to the Production Controller, Robin Freeley. Introduce yourself and your company. You want to arrange an appointment to talk about your products.

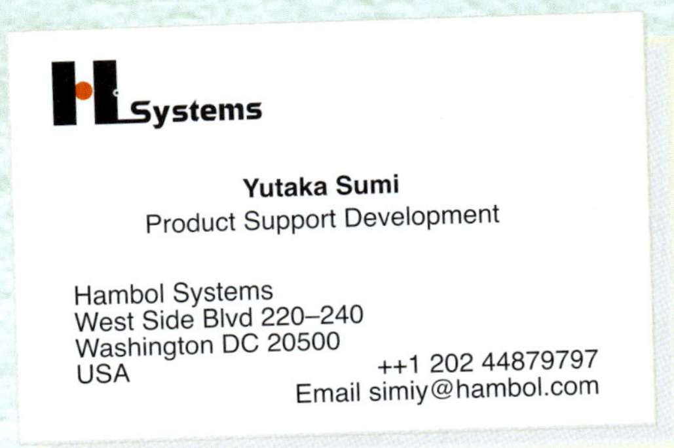

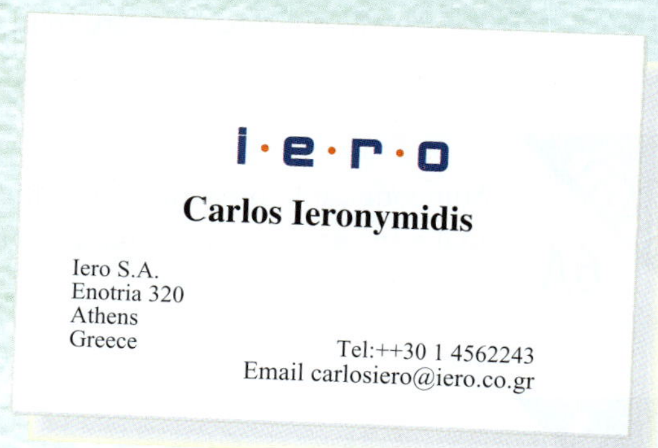

FILE CARD 13A

Your position in the discussion is basically to support investment in public transport. Do this by referring to:

- environmental benefits
- improvements in quality of life
- public transport is cheaper
- cars are heavy consumers of raw materials
- people want improved transport.

In the discussion:

- accept some interruptions but make sure you get all your arguments across
- defend your arguments
- be polite but firm
- repeat if necessary.

You start.

FILE CARD 8A

You are the Personal Assistant to your boss, Ken Siam. A caller rings to speak to him. Take down any details you need and promise to call back next week. Your boss is on holiday but you do not want to say this.

FILE CARD 11A

You are an Order Processor for Office Universe Limited, a London-based stationery and office equipment company. A customer rings with a problem over an invoice.

Here is a copy of the invoice:

Office Universe Limited
430–4 Upper Richmond Road
London SW15 5TY England
Telephone 0207 434 7272 Fax 0207 434 5286
www.officeuniverse.com
Email accounts@officeuniverse.co.uk

INVOICE

Angus Ltd
Galloway Industrial Estate North Side
Unit 15
Aberdeen AB24 5TR

Your ref: OOU22.10
Our ref: RG3472/5

Part ref	Qty	Item	Price
2356-1	100	A4 Zoom Copy Paper @ £2.20	£220.00
4563-1	2	packs Marker pens @ £5.80	£11.60
2156-2	1	Staples 5000 pack	£5.20
2134-8	20	Rulers @ £0.80	£16.00
3672-2	100	Coloured ring binders @ £2.10	£210.00
3482-1	100	Pack of dividers @ £0.56	£11.20

Sub-total	£473.00
Less discount 5%	£23.65
Sub-total	£449.35
VAT @ 17.5%	£78.64
Sub-total	£527.99
+ Carriage and packing £20 + £3.50 VAT @ 17.5%	£23.50
TOTAL	£551.49

Terms: 30 days from invoice date.
Thank you for your custom.
Telephone or fax your orders to Julie 24 hours a day, 365 days a year.

Notes:

- You have checked with the original telephoned order and can find no mistake: the customer did order all the goods you have sent. You do sell cheaper copy paper and cheaper ring binders, but with different part reference numbers.
- You accept the customer should have received a 10% discount and free carriage and packing – offer to send a new invoice.
- Your company recently altered its terms to 30 days for all customers and all were notified in a separate letter.
- You cannot take back the order but if the customer is unhappy he / she can return the goods and no fee will be charged.
- Offer to send different quality (standard, not laser quality) copy paper and different ring binders (plain coloured).

FILE CARD 10A

You are the same Quality Control Manager for Comcosol. You are in your office when the telephone rings.

FILE CARD 12A

Describe this graph to a colleague. Say what the subject of the picture is, then explain the details of the graph and highlight one or two key facts.

Fig. 1. Air Pollutants: emissions of selected gases

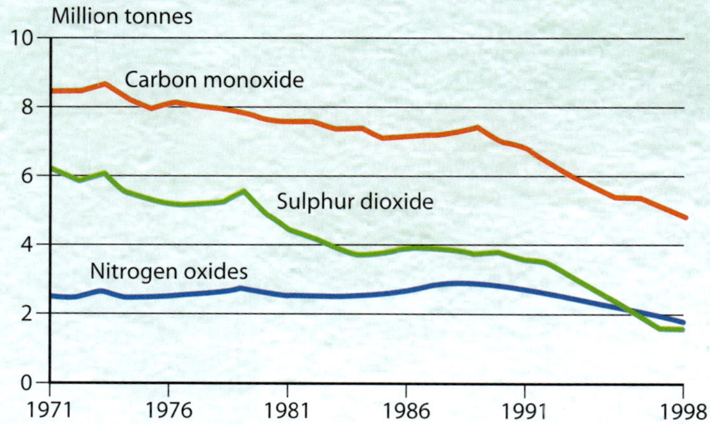

Source: ***Social Trends 2001*****. Crown Copyright 2001.**
Reproduced by permission of the Controller of HMSO and of the Office for National Statistics.

Later your partner will describe the graph below for you. You complete the missing details, asking questions if necessary.

Fig. 2. .... from fossil-fuel burning by economic region, 1950–95

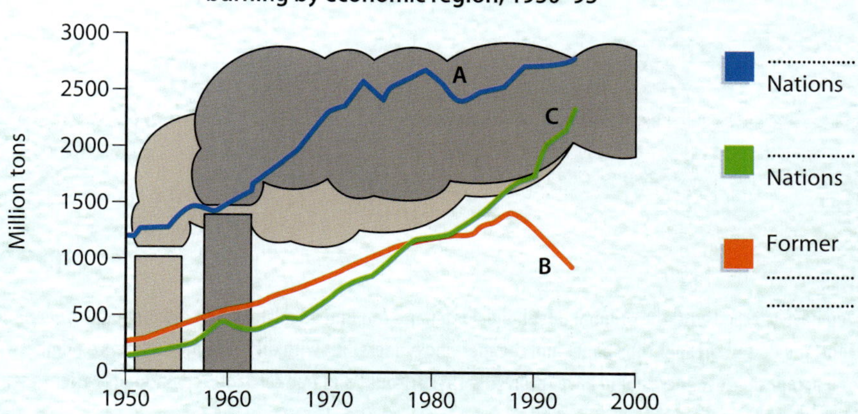

FILE CARD 3A

Your partner is a visitor to the town where you live and / or work. You would like to invite him / her to a social event or provide some entertainment. Think about the possibilities, then find out his / her preferences and make an arrangement with him / her.

Suggestion: Look in a local *What's On* guide or newspaper to see if there are any special attractions on now.

FILE CARD 9A

You are a Quality Control Manager for Comcosol, a software engineering company that supplies manufacturers with control systems. Ring one of your clients, Salco Services – and ask to speak to the Production Manager. You want an appointment to discuss some design modifications.

Here is a page from your diary. If possible you want to visit Salco the week of October 17th.

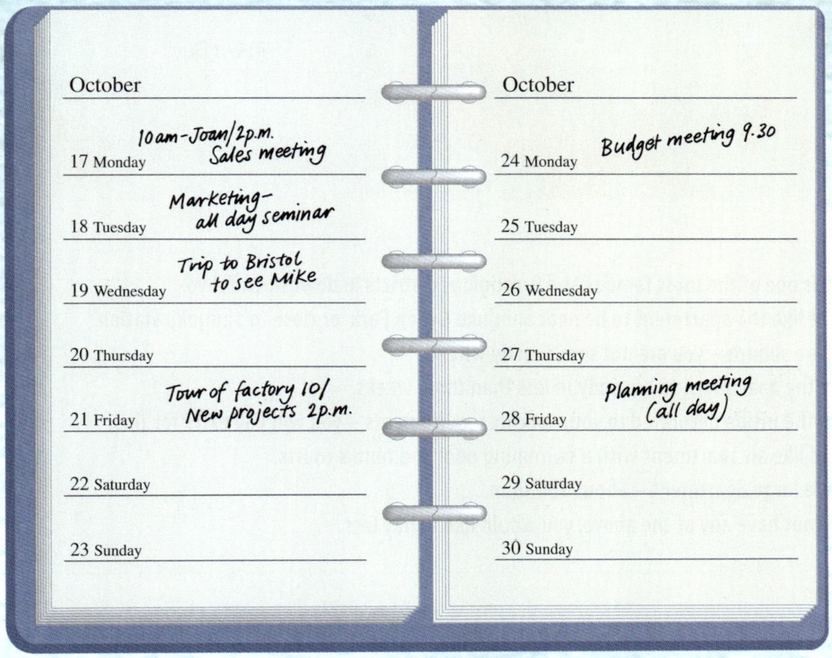

FILE CARD 15A

You are a sales representative for an advertising consultancy. You are responsible for selling perimeter advertising for sports arenas in Italy. You sell 25 metre electronic advertising at Italian Serie A (first division) football matches.

- Price: on live television:
  - corner position: $120 per flash (one minute)
  - halfway line or behind the goal $240 per flash (one minute)
- You can offer discounts of up to 20%, but only for deals of three matches or more.
- You can offer two free flashes at non-televised games instead of a discount.

Notes:

You have no space on the halfway line (middle of the playing area) in January and February.

A deal must be for a minimum of 10 flashes per match.

FILE CARD 16A

You represent an international company with business links in Tokyo. You urgently need to buy a brand-new luxury apartment in Tokyo's Shinjuku district.

You could spend up to ¥250m, but you would prefer to spend only about ¥150m because you would also like to buy a second, smaller apartment in Hachioji – but this is not essential.

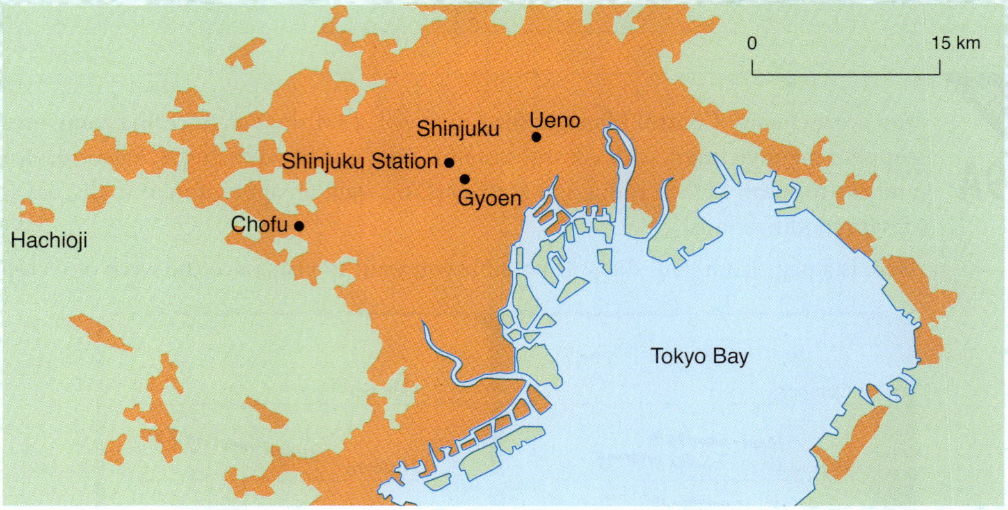

Notes:

- Shinjuku is one of the most famous and prestigious districts in downtown Tokyo.
- You would like the apartment to be near Shinjuku Gyoen Park, or close to Shinjuku station.
- Hachioji is a suburb – you are not sure exactly where.
- You need the apartment to be ready in less than three weeks.
- You want the inside decorated to your specific requirements – you will pay extra for this.
- You would like an apartment with a swimming pool and tennis courts.
- You want a large apartment – about 200 sq.m.
- If you cannot have any of the above, you would like to pay less.

FILE CARD 19A

Team A: HBT Rexis Ltd – a subsidiary of HBT Inc.

Your company has recently developed an anti-inflammatory drug to treat arthritis. You plan to market the drug within two years. You want to include your sister company, HBT Short Ltd., in the project because they have more experience in testing and marketing this type of drug. They already produce *Arpan*, an anti-arthritis drug with a large market share.

You:

- would like to set up a Project Team, based at Rexis. You think the team should consist of three members from Rexis and two from Short.
- expect the final development of the drug, including the trials and salaries (calculated in employee-hours) of Project Team members, will cost $900,000.
- have to apply for a patent for the drug and for it to be licensed by the American Food and Drug Administration. You expect approval within two years.

Note

If you cannot reach agreement, you plan to develop the drug alone.

FILE CARD **17A**

Team A: Coen Brothers

The negotiation. Clearly you would like to supply all three buildings to Fratelli Taviani, but be sure not to give away too much in terms of discount. Against this, it is very important that you enter the Italian market.

There are certain extras that you can provide at little extra cost: you can decorate the finished buildings and you can agree to an extended warranty of up to ten years. This means total building replacement in the event of structural faults developing. Ordinary maintenance and wear and tear is not included.

Discount	2%	4 points
	5%	3 points
	8%	2 points
	10%	1 point
	>10%	0 points
Delivery and completion of work	30 days	0 points
	60 days	1 point
	90 days	3 points
To pay all of delivery costs		0 points
To pay half of delivery costs		1 point
To pay no delivery costs		2 points
Payment over 12 months		−1 point
Payment over 6 months		2 points
Payment on completion		3 points
To offer complete free decoration		– point
Extended 10-year warranty		– point

FILE CARD **18A**

Situation 1

You work for a translation agency. You can translate legal contracts into any language:

- cost: $300 per 1,000 words
- a job of more than 5,000 words will take a week
- if it is more urgent than a week, the cost will be a lot higher.

Situation 2

You are in Hamburg. You urgently need to rent four vans from a local car and van rental company:

- you expect to pay about €100 per day per van
- you have to have the vans today or tomorrow.

Situation 3

You are the Conference Organiser for Lake View Hotel. You rent conference space:

- cost: normally $1,000 per day for facilities for five people
- 50% non-refundable deposit six months before the conference date (this is negotiable)
- bed and breakfast conference rate – another $1,000 per day for five people
- no deposit required for bed and breakfast.

File cards 1B to 19B

FILE CARD 4B

You receive a visitor to the town where you now live, or to your birthplace.

You agree to have a meal in a restaurant. *Either* use a menu from a local restaurant, printed in your own language (explain in English what the various dishes are), *or* use the menu below. Talk about what there is to eat, choose what to have, comment on the restaurant, talk about the town and the number of visitors, tourism, places of interest, etc.

If you like, develop small talk about business, work or the state of the country's economy and / or business prospects.

Act out parts of the meal. Comment on the food.

Finally, ask for the bill. *You* intend to pay – you are the host. Final comments on the meal. Decide what to do next.

MENU

Starter

Chilled Andaluz Gaspacho £3.50
A superb treat from Southern Spain. A cold soup rich in tomatoes, cucumber, parsley and garlic.

Roasted Piedmont Peppers £3.50
From Northern Italy. Two halves of red pepper filled with sun dried tomatoes and anchovies. Finished with basil and garlic.

Fish Soup £4.00
A rich broth of fish stock with whole prawns, squid and mussels.

Deep Fried Squid £4.00
Squid rings fried in a herb batter and served with a light salad.

Field Mushrooms with Garlic £4.50
An Italian speciality. A steaming hot dish of quality porcini in oil and garlic.

Salmon and Dill £4.50
A Norwegian treat. Smoked salmon from the northern fjords. Served with dill and a chunk of lemon.

Cream of Vegetable Soup £3.50
Fresh vegetables in a rich broth topped with cream.

Tomato Salad with Garlic and Herbs £3.00
Succulent tomatoes dressed in extra virgin olive oil with chives and basil.

Mixed Basque Salad £4.00
From the Basque region of Spain. Asparagus, lettuce, tomatoes, onion and queen olives topped with chunks of tuna fish and egg.

Main Course

Fish

Sea Bream Plaki £17.00
A Greek speciality. A meaty white fish cooked in tomato and onion sauce with lemon and coriander. Served on a bed of rice.

Rainbow Trout with Herbs £15.00
Fresh trout baked in the oven with rosemary and thyme. Served with new potatoes or rice.

Hake with Cockles £15.00
Fresh hake steak fried in oil with cockles and parsley giving the typical salsa verde of the Basque region of Spain.

Thai Fish Cakes with Curry Sauce £15.00
A hot and spicy treat from Thailand. White fish cooked with lime, ginger and lemon grass and served with a spicy sauce.

Grilled Seafood £17.00
A mixture of grilled prawns, cockles, mussels, shrimps and squid, served with garlic bread and salad.

Meat

Sirloin Steak £15.00
Grilled sirloin cooked to your specifications and garnished with butter and parsley. Served with new potatoes.

Fillet Steak £17.00
Grilled fillet steak cooked to your specifications and garnished with butter and parsley. Served with new potatoes.

Roast Lamb £15.00
Oven baked shoulder or leg of lamb with garlic and rosemary. Served with new potatoes.

Spiced Lamb and Cashew Kebabs £14.00
Barbecued chunks of lamb with onions, peppers and cashew nuts. Served with rice.

Rabbit Hot Pot £14.00
A superb stew of rabbit cooked in a rich broth of onions, stout and prunes. Served with baked potatoes.

Chicken with Sherry Vinegar and Tarragon Sauce £14.00
A classic French recipe, fried and served in a deep earthenware dish, with new potatoes.

Chicken Stir Fry £16.00
Chicken breast lightly fried in a rich assortment of chopped vegetables.

Vegetarian

Rigatoni with Asparagus *au Gratin* £14.00
Fresh pasta with asparagus and a cheese topping.

Roasted Vegetables with Couscous £14.00
A colourful assortment of fresh vegetables served with feta cheese on a bed of couscous.

Spaghetti with Oil, Chilli Peppers and Parmesan £12.00
A classic pasta dish from Italy, with a garlic-enhanced olive oil sauce, spiced with dried chillis. Served with fresh Parmesan cheese.

Lasagne Bake £14.00
The classic vegetarian lasagne with layers of fresh pasta in a white sauce with mixed vegetables, mozzarella and Parmesan cheese.

Dessert

All desserts £4.50

Strawberry meringue with ice cream
Apple and apricot tart
Summer fruits cheesecake
Chocolate cake with cream
Caramel flan
Fruit of the day
Fresh fruit salad
Ice creams

FILE CARD 1B

You have just arrived at D.F.M., a London-based pharmaceuticals company. You have an appointment to see Rowena Stanton in the Research Department.

You are very busy and have another appointment this afternoon and one in Manchester tomorrow. It would actually suit you to spend some time preparing for these appointments.

Note:

- **Be prepared to engage in a few minutes' small talk with the person looking after you.**
- **You would like to prepare for your meeting this afternoon.**
- **You would like a recommendation on what would be a nice gift for your partner (male or female) back home.**
- **You would like to send and receive a confidential fax.**

FILE CARD 2B

You are expecting a visitor from Caldos, a multinational company with a plant in Germany. You have arranged a meeting to talk about the products and services you offer. You have sent your visitor an outline plan for the day.

Welcome the visitor and spend a few minutes making him / her feel relaxed. There are at present strikes affecting trains and buses in your region of the country. The roads are likely to be congested.

Finally suggest that you go to meet one of your colleagues, Bert Trautman.

FILE CARD 3B

You are visiting your partner in the town where he / she lives and / or works. He / she wants to arrange some social event or entertainment for you. Make an arrangement with him/her.

FILE CARD 5B

Someone calls to talk to your boss, Andrea Koss. Ask the caller to spell his / her name / company name so you can write it down. Andrea Koss is not available – she is in a meeting and cannot be disturbed. Offer to take a message or say she will call back – later today.

If you plan to ask Andrea to call back, get a phone number.

FILE CARD 6B

Choose one of the identities given below. Call your partner to ask if you can visit him / her and try to make an arrangement today. You want to talk about his / her company's products.

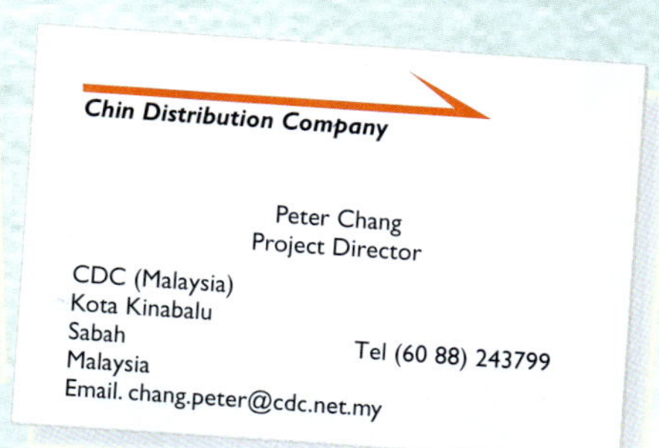

FILE CARD 7B

You are the secretary to Robin Freeley, Production Controller at Hamwell Ltd. Your boss is busy and cannot be disturbed. Deal with the caller and do not disturb your boss!

FILE CARD 8B

Choose one of the identities shown below:

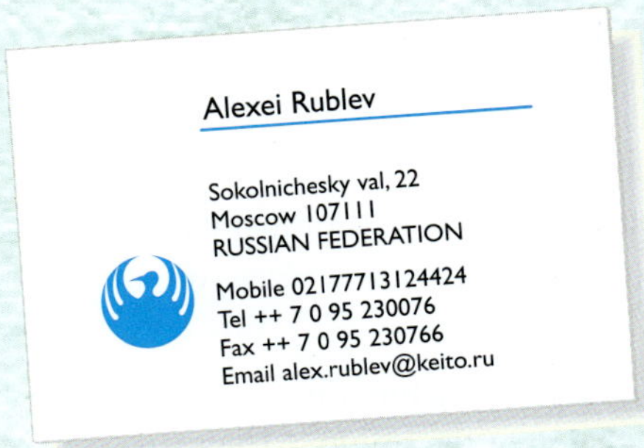

Ring a Japanese contact called Ken Siam. You would like to meet him to talk about the potential of your products.

FILE CARD 9B

You are Production Manager at Salco Services. A supplier, Comcosol Ltd., telephones you. Here is an extract from your diary.

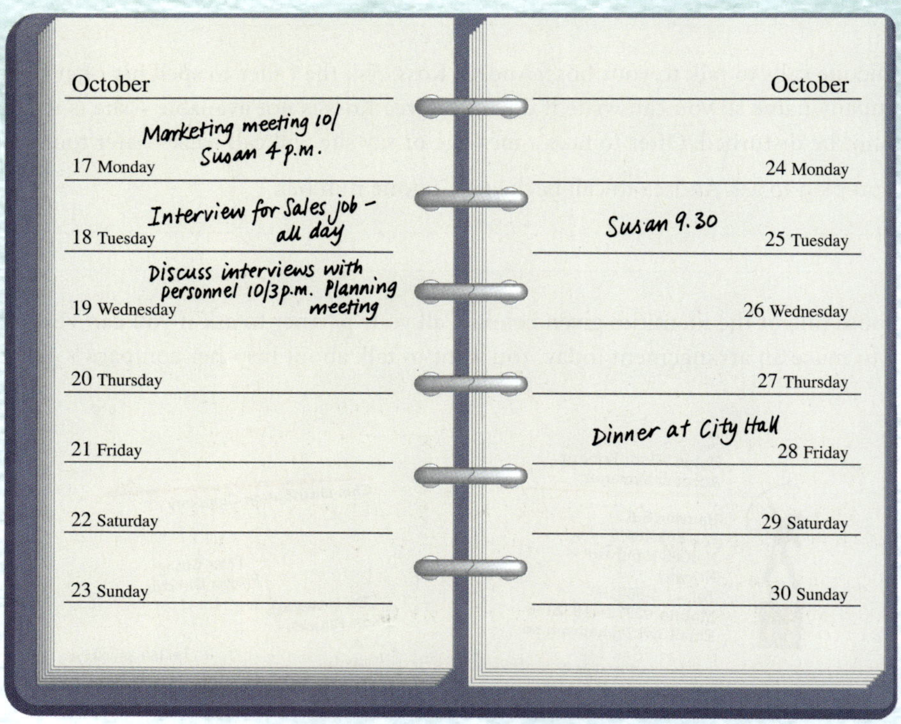

FILE CARD **11B**

You have bought office equipment and stationery supplies from a company called Office Universe Ltd. Unfortunately there have been problems with the service. Here is a copy of the invoice they sent you for the last order:

Office Universe Limited
430–4 Upper Richmond Road
London SW15 5TY England
Telephone 0207 434 7272 Fax 0207 434 5286
www.officeuniverse.com
Email accounts@officeuniverse.co.uk

INVOICE

Angus Ltd
Galloway Industrial Estate North Side
Unit 15
Aberdeen AB24 5TR

Your ref: OOU22.10
Our ref: RG3472/5

Part ref	Qty	Item	Price
2356-1	100	A4 Zoom Copy Paper @ £2.20	£220.00
4563-1	2	packs Marker pens @ £5.80	£11.60
2156-2	1	Staples 5000 pack	£5.20
2134-8	20	Rulers @ £0.80	£16.00
3672-2	100	Coloured ring binders @ £2.10	£210.00
3482-1	100	Pack of dividers @ £0.56	£11.20

Sub-total	£473.00
Less discount 5%	£23.65
Sub-total	£449.35
VAT @ 17.5%	£78.64
Sub-total	£527.99
+ Carriage and packing £20 + £3.50 VAT @ 17.5%	£23.50
TOTAL	£551.49

Terms: 30 days from invoice date.

Thank you for your custom.

Telephone or fax your orders to Julie 24 hours a day, 365 days a year.

Notes:

- **The company normally give you 10% discount and normal terms are 60 days from invoice.**
- **The OU catalogue offered ring binders at £1.50 and A4 copy paper at £1.45.**
- **They do not usually charge for carriage or packing on orders of over £200.00.**
- **You did not order any staples.**
- **You have used OU in the past and have had problems with wrong deliveries.**
- **Ask for your order to be despatched again and the wrong order taken away.**
- **Ask for a new invoice.**
- **Be prepared to say you will use other suppliers in future.**

FILE CARD **10B**

You are still the Production Manager at Salco Services. A day after your conversation with Comcosol, you learn that you have to go to Japan on urgent business to discuss a legal problem. Unfortunately you must change your appointment with Comcosol.

Telephone Comcosol. Try to fix an appointment for the following week – when you have no commitments.

Write a fax to confirm the new arrangement.

FILE CARD **12B**

Listen to your colleague describing this graph. Write the missing information. Ask any questions you want.

Fig. 1 ....

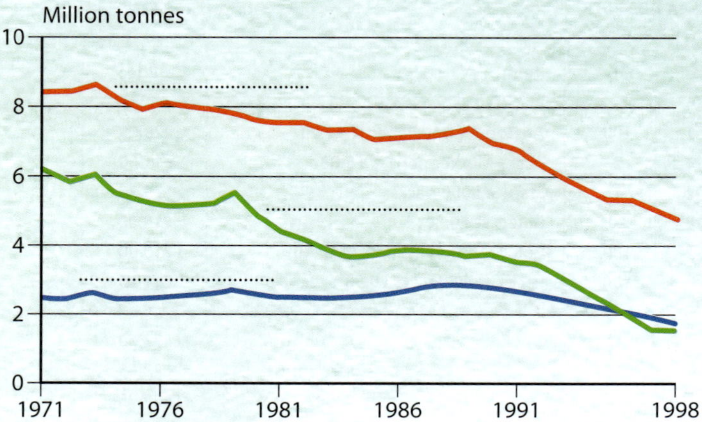

Source: *Social Trends 2001*. **Crown Copyright 2001.**

Reproduced by permission of the Controller of HMSO and of the Office for National Statistics.

Now you describe this graph. Begin by saying what the picture represents, then explain the details. Highlight any especially important information.

Fig. 2 Carbon emissions from fossil-fuel burning by economic region, 1950-95

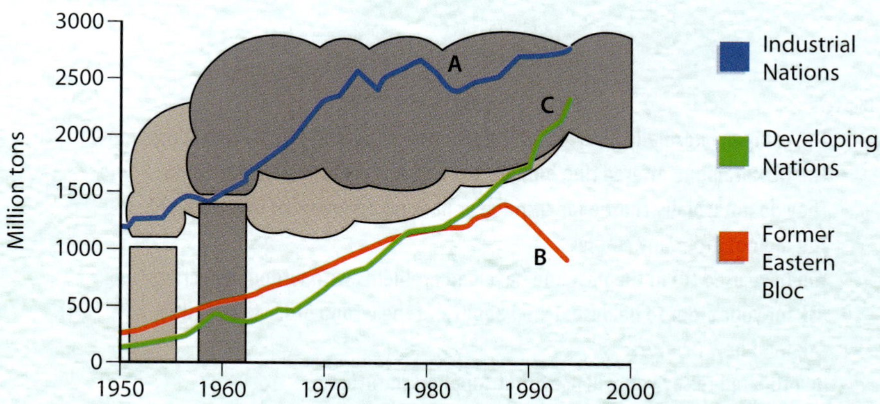

FILE CARD 13B

Your position is to defend the freedom of private car ownership. You think:

- quality of life depends on freedom of choice
- people want personal space – cars make this possible
- people want to leave and to arrive when they want
- public transport is massively expensive, through taxation
- the car industry employs many thousands of people.

In the discussion:

- oppose simplistic arguments for the expansion of public transport
- interrupt when you think your colleague says something simplistic or wrong
- present the arguments above
- be polite, but firm.

Your partner will start.

FILE CARD 14B

Team B: Fratelli Taviani. You are representatives of Fratelli Taviani, an Italian agricultural feeds manufacturer. You have a meeting with Coen Brothers, a London-based Anglo-Dutch company.

Your requirements. You need to build a new office and storage buildings at your Asti plant in Piedmont, in Northern Italy. There are many suppliers of prefabricated industrial buildings.

You need two standard-quality storage buildings with electricity, water and air-conditioning systems. You also need an office building of the highest quality. You expect to have the buildings decorated at extra cost by a local decorator.

You want the buildings to be supplied and erected within 30 days, but you could allow 60 days.

The market. You would like to use a local supplier, Daniele Edili, who supplied some of your existing buildings. Unfortunately they are on average 10% more expensive than Coen Brothers. Coen products are also better quality. On the other hand, Coen is a new company and you need assurances on their quality and ability to meet deadlines.

FILE CARD 18B

Situation 1

You want a legal contract translated into English:

- it is 6,000 words long
- you expect to pay between $1,200 and $1,500
- you need it in two days – three days maximum.

Situation 2

You are a car and van rental company in Hamburg:

- van rental costs €120 per day
- 10% discount for orders over €1,000
- no vans are available today and only two tomorrow.

Situation 3

You want to rent conference space at the Lake View Hotel:

- find out the cost for ten people for your two-day sales conference in eight months' time
- ask for a discount
- ask if you have to pay a deposit
- insist that it is refundable.

FILE CARD 15B

You represent an international fashion house with a major youth market, especially in Italy and Spain. You want to advertise at Italian Serie A (first division) football matches. You have a budget of $10,000. You would like the following:

- electronic advertising at matches on live television only
- a minimum of ten flashes in every game (a flash = one minute)
- you prefer halfway line positions (they are most often seen by the TV cameras)
- you don't want behind the goal unless you get a good discount
- you would like to advertise at between four and six matches in the early part of the year (January–March).

FILE CARD 16B

You represent an international property company. You are selling luxury apartments in Tokyo.

Costs:	Shinjuku district	Y100m to Y200m
	Ueno	Y70m to Y80m
	Hachioji	Y60m
	Chofu	Y80m

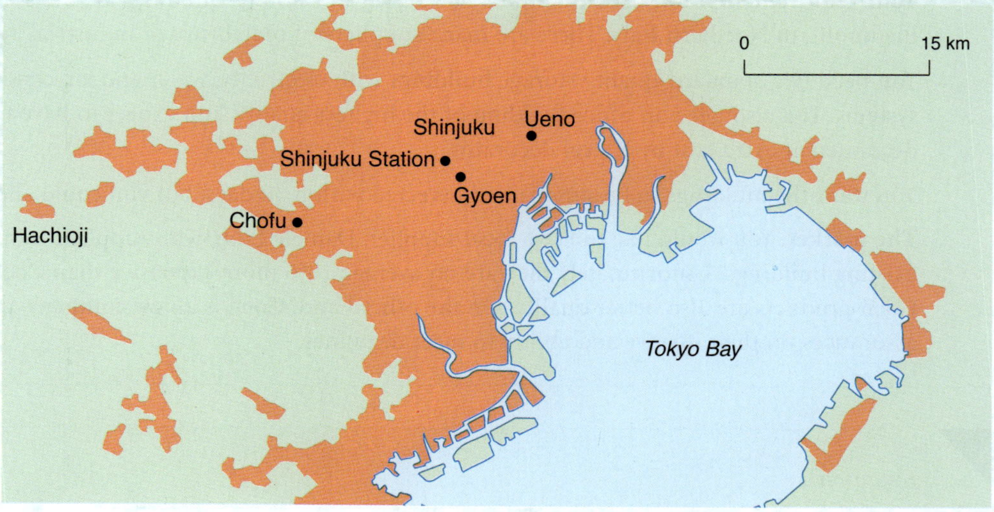

Notes:

- **Apartments in Tokyo are small: land is very expensive.**
- **70 sq.m is normal, 100 sq.m is large by Tokyo standards.**
- **It is virtually impossible to provide a swimming pool or tennis courts.**
- **You have two new apartments in Shinjuku:**
  - **100 sq.m at ¥120m**
  - **150 sq.m, near the Shinjuku Gyoen Park, ¥200m.**
- **Shinjuku is one of the most famous and prestigious districts in downtown Tokyo.**
- **Prices are negotiable – but no more than 20% less.**
- **Hachioji is a suburb, about 40 minutes by train from the centre.**
- **You have an excellent apartment in Chofu (nearer the centre) for sale at ¥120m.**
- **The apartments could be ready in 5 to 6 weeks.**
- **Special interior designs can be arranged – cost about ¥20m.**

FILE CARD 17B

Team B: Fratelli Taviani

The negotiation. You would like to buy all three buildings from the one supplier, but if you do this you expect a good discount and favourable delivery and payment terms.

You have received the following confidential information:

fratelli taviani s.p.a.

INTERNAL MEMO—CONFIDENTIAL

To: Purchasing Dept
From: DA

Daniele Edill prices are up 10% on last year – a common trend in the Italian prefabricated building sector. Consider buying outside Italy – quality guarantees must equal those available in Italy – i.e. 3 years' free maintenance.
Suggest looking for this in any contract agreed with Coen Brothers.

Discount	2%	1 point
	5%	2 points
	8%	3 points
	10%	4 points
Delivery and completion of work	30 days	3 points
	60 days	1 point
	90 days	0 points
To pay all of delivery costs		0 points
To pay half of delivery costs		1 point
To pay no delivery costs		2 points
Payment over 12 months		3 points
Payment over 6 months		2 points
Payment on completion		–1 point
1-year warranty		0 points
2-year warranty		1 point
3-year warranty		2 points
10-year warranty		3 points

FILE CARD 19B

Team B: HBT Short Ltd. – a subsidiary of HBT Inc.

Your colleagues in a sister subsidiary, HBT Rexis Ltd., have asked you to participate in the development and marketing of a new drug to treat arthritis.

You:

- are experienced in this sector of the drug industry
- presently market *Arpan*, which has 25% of the domestic market and a growing export market
- would like to cooperate with Rexis, because you do not want to compete with them in the arthritis drug market
- need to be flexible in negotiating with them
- do not believe a single Project Team is required. You think there should be one team in charge of the tests, based at Rexis, and one team in charge of marketing, based at Short
- think that $500,000 is the *absolute maximum* that should be spent on developing the drug
- are sceptical about its market potential. You feel that it could simply take sales away from *Arpan*. The following memo was written following a meeting of your Product Development Executive:

HBT Short Ltd.: Internal Memo

CONFIDENTIAL

Re. Arpan / New Rexis anti-inflammatory drug

This Rexis product could be a threat to ARPAN.
Development should avoid high investment, especially by Short.
Some commitment is acceptable, but … keep costs down!

Product Development Executive

- think further tests will take at least three years before the American Food and Drug Administration give approval
- would prefer that Short take responsibility for the trials and in exchange you will provide information about potential markets once the tests have been completed.

File cards 20 to 33

FILE CARD **20**

Staff consultation on leisure facilities in the workplace

The company has money to spend on improving facilities for staff.
Among the options are:

- a sports club with new gym and bar facilities
- a crèche and after-school centre for employees' children
- a swimming pool and café area
- a bar / restaurant / library / Internet café for staff and families

Decide on priorities. Suggest a recommendation based on one of the above, or a combination of two.

FILE CARD **21**

High turnover of staff in Daycare Centre

Total employees: 300
170 women
45 are mothers with young children

Company daycare facilities for children are used:

- after school before the end of the working day
- in school holidays

Parents are unhappy because:

- very high turnover of staff in the centre
- no continuity
- poor organisation of the Centre

FILE CARD **22**

Loss of car parking spaces

Because of a large expansion of office and production space, most staff car parking will soon disappear. How should the company distribute the 100 spaces that are left?

Note: **the company employs about 300 staff**
about 28 staff are disabled
the company is located on bus and train routes
about 200 staff currently use car parking space at work

FILE CARD 23

Policy on contemporary artwork for reception area

The company has always supported contemporary art with regular purchasing and exhibition of paintings and sculpture. It now has quite a good collection of over 100 pieces. Only about a third of the collection is on display.

There are arguments about what to do with the collection and about the purchase and exhibition policy. Are there other more important priorities for the company?

Options:

- Sell the work and stop buying art
- Build a gallery to exhibit the work
- Donate the work to the local City Art Gallery & Museum
- Stay as now, showing some work in the reception area, changing the works occasionally, but buying no more.

FILE CARD 24

Sam Adela (Chair)

You have called a meeting of the Executive of Adela Passam Ltd. to discuss the crisis surrounding the company. Prepare a brief agenda and short opening remarks. Refer to the Checklists in Unit 10 to remind you of your responsibilities as Chair and some of the language you may need.

You:

- are the most heavily implicated in the scandal
- are a friend of Cass
- are angry that the press allege that your late father, Mikel Adela, may have profited by up to $1m from Cass's deal
- think APL should sue the local papers for libel.

FILE CARD 25

Jay Worthy (Legal Advisor to APL)

You:

- are worried that the accusations may be true but you cannot say this directly
- think APL should wait and see what happens next
- feel that the scandal really involved Cass and politicians but …
- you cannot say this too loudly because Marta Lucas is married to the former leader of the Democratic People's Party.

Note: From a legal point of view, probably no individual has been libelled because no one has been named in the reports except Mikel Adela who is now dead and the dead cannot be libelled.

FILE CARD 26

Marta Lucas (Director)

You:

- have never heard of the scandal until very recently but your husband is deeply embarrassed
- believe your position with the company is compromised if your husband is found to be corrupt
- think that if you resign, it will look like an admission of guilt
- may decide that on the other hand, your relationship with your husband is compromised!
- believe the company should fight to protect its – and your – reputation.

FILE CARD 27

Anton Hassim (Director)

You:

- fear that the public will make direct connections based on Sam Adela's friendship with Cass and Marta Lucas's marriage to the leader of the Democratic People's Party
- think that even if Sam Adela did not benefit personally, if people think Mikel Adela was guilty, then the company is in deep trouble
- think the company should wait, admit nothing and deny nothing
- think that to sue the papers for libel is risky and would cost a fortune.

FILE CARD 28

Pat Joyce (Director)

You:

- feel that the allegations must be completely false because you knew Mikel Adela for forty years as a completely honest man
- believe that APL never had any formal dealings with politics and politicians
- think Marta Lucas's personal life is her own affair
- think the company should issue a statement denying the allegations, publish accounts from the period, etc.

FILE CARD 29

Berni Callam (Accountant)

You:

- are new in Adela Passam and you are shocked by the scandal
- naturally hope that the accusations are false and that the affair only involves the Council and Cass
- feel that a thorough independent investigation of the accounts should clear the company's reputation
- want to avoid a legal battle
- fear that the public will always associate Cass with Adela Passam and with Mikel and Sam Adela
- think that in time the damage will fade
- think every company has its scandals.

FILE CARD 30

Jan Lubitsch (Managing Director and Chair)

Introduce the background and the problem. Explain that the promotion has been oversubscribed (you forecasted 1,000 takers, and there are 5,000). You fear that the costs of meeting the extra 4,000 will be enormous. The problem is that Blue Balloon do not have the capacity and anyway are contracted only to provide 1,000 trips at £80.

During the discussion, you want to establish what action should be taken. Set specific actions that must be done after the meeting.

FILE CARD 31

Andrew / Andrea Eastman (Marketing Director)

You feel ultimately responsible because you decided to run the promotion. You insured Sola against oversubscription but only up to 1,000 extra trips, not 4,000. You took advice from an advertising agency, Promo World. You feel they gave you wrong advice and Sola should seek compensation from them.

FILE CARD 32

Fred / Freda Cavani (Director)

You think Sola were wrongly advised and should receive compensation from the advertising agency, Promo World, who advised Sola on the promotion. You want to know what the legal position is on getting compensation.

FILE CARD 33

Eric / Erica Whitehead (Director)

You think Blue Balloon should fix up more balloon trips at a cheaper price than £80, or that other companies could be approached to help out. You are concerned about the bad publicity around the promotion. You think Promo World should explain why they thought insurance for only 1,000 extra trips would be enough. However, you also think the situation cannot be so serious, as clearly many hundreds of people stayed in your hotels and may return for a second visit – so perhaps it has been a good promotion after all. You imagine that Promo World will say that, anyway.

For Judith, Ruth and Neil
with love from Dad.

Acknowledgements

The author is grateful to Pamela Rogerson-Revell for help with the first edition and to colleagues and friends at York Associates for ideas, resources and piloting the material. Thanks are due to colleagues at Cambridge University Press, including Peter Donovan and Sarah Almy, and to James Dale, who suggested many improvements and prepared the manuscript for production. Special thanks go to Will Capel, who provided unstinting support, essential advice and encouragement. Finally, thanks to Carolyn Parsons for preparing the second edition manuscript for production.

The author and publishers would like to thank the following institutions and teachers for their help in piloting and commenting on the material and for the invaluable feedback which they provided.

Mary Crowe, Insearch Language Centre, Sydney, Australia. Keith Hanna, Stuttgart, Germany. Carol Herrmann, Sindelfingen, Germany. Andy Cresswell, The British Institute of Florence, Italy. Mark Baker, International House, La Spezia, Italy. Teresa Yolanda Mustion de Garcia, University of Guadalajara, Mexico.

The author and publishers are grateful to the following copyright owners for permission to reproduce copyright material. Every endeavour has been made to contact copyright owners and apologies are expressed for any omissions.

pp. 6 and 7: From *Managing Cultural Differences, Fourth Edition*, by Philip R. Harris and Robert T. Moran. Copyright © 1996 by Gulf Publishing Company, Houston, Texas. Used with permission. All rights reserved.
p. 14: From *Riding the Waves of Culture: Understanding Cultural Diversity in Business* by Fons Trompenaars. Nicholas Brealey Publishing Ltd, London, 1993.
pp. 35, 45 and 46: From *Faxes, phones and foreigners* with the kind permission of British Telecommunications plc.
pp. 66 and 104: From *The Handbook of Communication Skills* by Bernice Hurst. London: Kogan Page, 1991.
pp. 116 and 121: From *Better Meeting Skills* by Marion Haynes. London: Kogan Page, 1988.
pp. 69, 158 and 166: Source: *Social Trends 2001*. Office for National Statistics. Crown Copyright 2001. Reproduced by permission of the Controller of HMSO and of the Office for National Statistics.
pp. 96 and 133: From *The Gower Handbook of Management*. Aldershot: Gower, 1988.
p. 96: © Milo O. Frank 1989. Extracted from *How to Run a Successful Meeting in Half the Time* published by Corgi, a division of Transworld Publishers Ltd. All rights reserved. Reprinted with the permission of Simon & Schuster.

The authors and publishers are grateful to the following illustrators and photographic sources:

Illustrators:
p65 Kathy Baxendale; pp. 1, 4, 37, 74 and 95 Peter Byatt; pp. 3, 8, 13, 43 and 73 Paul Chappell; p. 27 Paul Dickinson; pp. 25 and 29 Matthew Doyle; p. 52 Clive Goodyer; pp. 46, 51, 52, 62, 72, 86, 106, 120 and 122 Edward McLachlan; pp. 16, 17, 21, 25, 39, 48, 67, 80, 89, 90, 98, 105, 111, 138 and 148 Oxford Illustrators Ltd; pp. 45 and 124 Oxprint Design Ltd.; p. 57 Jennifer Ward; p.125 Jonathan Williams.

Photographers/Photographic sources:
p. 106 Ace Photo Agency; p. 8b W. Capel; p. 124b Corbis/W. Hodges; p. 11l L. Hunter/J. Dale; pp. 5, 6t, 14t Image Bank/W. Bibikow, p. 11r Image Bank/D. Paul Productions, p. 15tl Image Bank/Chabruken, p. 42 Image Bank/Real Life, pp. 95, 96t & l, 103t, 113t Image Bank/S. Lindberg, p. 96r Image Bank/R. Lockyer, p. 105l Image Bank/D. Hummel, p. 118b Image Bank/J. Cadge; p. 8t ImageState Pictor, p. 11mb ImageState Pictor, p. 106tl ImageState Pictor, p. 118tl & 118tr, ImageState Pictor, p.128 ImageState Pictor; p. 38 Network Photographers/W. Kunz/Bilderberg, p. 105r Network Photographers/H. Gloaguen/Rapho, p. 106br Network Photographers/B. Lewis, p 106tr Network Photographers/H. J. Burkard/Bilderberg; p. 87r Powerstock, pp. 123, 124t, 132t, 142t Powerstock; p. 78 Science Photo Library; p. 6b Stone/S. Peters, p. 15tr Stone/P. Correz, p. 15br Stone/S. Grandadam, p. 19 Stone/T. Latham, p. 25t Stone/Prof. S. Lowther, p. 25b Stone/J. Darell, p. 47l Stone/J. polillio, p. 47r Stone/R. Roth, p. 55b Stone/D. Bosler, p. 88 Stone/L. Monneret, p. 118bl Stone/J. Gray, p. 119 Stone/R. Rusing; p. 11mt Taxi/V.C.L, p. 15bl Taxi/S. Simpson, p. 87l Taxi/V.C.L., pp. 23, 24t, 34t, 45t Taxi/P. Viant, p. 25mt Taxi/M. Goldman, p. 25mb Taxi/M. Malyszko, pp. 54, 55t, 64t, 76t, 86t Taxi/R. Brimson, p. 96bm Taxi/G. Buss.

(*l* = left, *r* = right, *t* = top, *b* = bottom)

Picture research by Hilary Fletcher with new additions by Mark Ruffle.